In Search of
Silence

Dropping the Baggage
Discovering what's REAL

Dear Hai

Thank you for being such
an inspiration.

with love & a heartfelt-
Namaste

Rohan

ROHAN NARSE

In Search of Silence

First published in 2011 by Ecademy Press

48 St Vincent Drive, St Albans, Hertfordshire, AL1 5SJ

info@ecademy-press.com www.ecademy-press.com

Printed and Bound by Lightning Source in the UK and USA

Set by Neil Coe

Printed on acid-free paper from managed forests. This book is printed on demand, so no copies will be remaindered or pulped.

ISBN 978-1-907722-51-6

To Jai and Tanya
for the wisdom and energy that you so embody
for the million moments of laughter together
for the gift of your presence
for your love

Acknowledgements

I am deeply indebted to...

- the two most beautiful women in my life: my grandmother Anusuya and my sister Yogita, fully present when it mattered the most, a presence beyond words and unconditional love at its best
- my aunt Lalitha, who got me started on writing and on expressing my heart
- the lighthouse in my life, Poonam, steady in the midst of the storm
- the artist of many a simple heartfelt conversation, Shivangi, authentic and total
- the sage within the family, Baba
- my dear friends, Dnyanesh, Ajay, Manoj, Bhuvanesh and their wives. Blessed by your presence
- my lovely Bengali brethren, Ranjana, Som, Bhargav and Sher. Blessed by your love and the effortless nature of our relationship. A meal at your home is such a celebration
- my batchmates from AFAC, IT BHU, IIM Bangalore and my former colleagues at the Tata Group, Coopers & Lybrand, KMPG, Goldman Sachs. You were all perfect mirrors reflecting what you saw and in that, I recognised who I was occurring as
- Neelesh, for those priceless moments of real gut-wrenching laughter, including the ones when reading 'The Book of Liff'
- Raj, for your presence, trust and support
- all those who were supportive, Ketan, Hiten, Kenny, and Rob, accommodative and patient when it was needed. A heartfelt namaste
- Kashyap, Atul, Pratik and the guys at Sunshine, showing how one can run a business with integrity; both heart and mind
- Bohman, for all the heartfelt chats
- David Alberto, a man with a large heart and a friend for life
- Karina, for being the first believer in the new journey
- David Heslop, for your wisdom and your love
- Rajesh, Dhiren, for our friendship over the years

- Brene Brown, you are an inspiration yourself
- Apple Inc, for nirvana in action, allowing me to experience flow
- Sona Laila, for the gift of a sparkling conversation with laughter to match
- Sarita, Luba and Leora, femininity personified in an increasingly masculine world
- the countless sanyasins and seekers that I met; I carry you in my heart
- those lovely souls I met along the way, co-travellers, shop keepers, car drivers, restaurant helpers, all those who just remained in the background
- Mohit, Shilpa and Isha and the magical meeting at the Jaisalmer fort, for listening, sharing and connecting at a level that was just perfect
- the people of Jaisalmer and those in the Golden Fort, a place where time is of no consequence
- Subbu, Ravi and Kavitha and the walk around Arunachala with you all
- Mooji, Adyashanti, Gangaji, Ken Wilber, Eckhart Tolle for all the satsangs over the years
- Ramana Maharishi, Papaji, Adi Da, Osho for the gift of your seeing
- Varanasi, a home away from home
- my teacher in Varanasi: simplicity, serenity and the wisdom of the ages. For the road back home to myself
- and finally, my parents. Without you, all this would have been a non-starter. What more can I say?

Introduction

Life, living it without being in a conscious state, is like starting a book in the middle. The beginning is not known and the constant desire to know what comes next prevents a real taste of the present. Birth, death and a 'dash' in the middle. That gap is filled with needless pursuits, momentary highs, a constant state of anxiety and an unexpressed sense of incompleteness. Freedom, health and relationships get traded for the mundane. The illusion is pursued to its fullest. Without realising, a raft of addictions then take hold. What a colossal waste of an opportunity to wake up!

My life mirrored this state totally and rather than start from the very beginning, here is how it was a few years ago. An ex-investment banker at Goldman Sachs living the 'high-life' in London, I had just quit to start an investment advisory business, raised the required capital and was in the process of closing deals, making money and further 'living the dream'. Qualifying in the best engineering and business school exams earlier in my life ensured that the pathway to the best firms, the best career opportunities and the rest was easier. To add to that was a deep survival-based instinct of wanting to win, no matter what the situation. The picture was perfect: living in London, global travel, a BMW, a TAG-HEUER and at times a Cartier on the wrist, holidays every year across the world, fine wines and sampling of the best of cuisine, cricket in London, tennis sessions, a personal trainer at times, scuba diving and rock-climbing, gliding, two lovely kids, a very supportive wife, happy parents and a seemingly ideal state for the next phase of life. Life was linear as every year brought more stuff. I was also growing older and it seemed natural just to be on the treadmill for everyone was doing the same. However, somewhere, something was not right, that was clear. Sleep patterns were becoming abnormal for no reason, the sense of distrust with the world at large was becoming increasingly evident, relationships with those close were becoming distant and health, which until some point was perfect, was giving way to short and at times longer bouts of sickness such as laryngitis, lower back pain and chronic muscle cramps. The separation between me and everything around was becoming bigger and bigger.

The part-time reading of 'self-help' books, the practice of yoga and pranayam, the adoption of various meditative techniques proposed by Masters on the path from dynamic meditations to vipasana, and regular gym sessions were helpful, but only just. All that seemed like allopathic medicine, much like taking OTC pills: good for a while for they suppressed the symptoms and life moved on, but deep down the discomfort remained that something was amiss. In spite of having climbed many a mountain, there was always a sense of incompletion; an unresolved and a deeply uncomfortable state. The dreams that I was living and fulfilling were not mine; a million unanswered questions about my life were still looming large and an inner zest for life itself seemed missing. In spite of all that was available, life felt totally unlived. This was supposed to be life as I heard and saw it in the expression of others. The older people I met, those who had worked their life in the corporate world pursuing dreams and fulfilling dreams, seemed lost and incomplete themselves and it was clear that any more of the same for me seemed untenable, for those ahead did not inspire confidence. In the midst of all the accumulated baggage, I really did not know who I was.

Then the biggest blessing in a long, long time happened – an accident, on the M25 in London (a busy ring road circling the city) as I was coming back from a meditation program organised in the English countryside. Tired from a whole day of cathartic and silent meditative techniques, I remember driving at about 70 miles per hour. The straight road to the M25, the M3, was OK for even a slight nap at the wheel wasn't such an issue. On the M25, the road was curved and, in a matter of a few minutes, I heard a loud bang, smelt gun-powder (nitrogen charge I am told, to get the air-bags to work) and the feel of glass on my face and neck. The hazard lights had come on, the car controls had taken over and it was impossible to accelerate. Just then I saw a 16-wheel trailer from behind, honking, powder coming out of its wheels as it tried to break to avoid a collision. There was nothing I could do but just watch, just be. The car edged slowly to the other side of the road, the hard shoulder, and the trailer missed it by a small margin. The car hit the hard shoulder and came to rest and I felt a trickle down the right side of my forehead, a head injury perhaps, I thought, but it was the black tea cup in the tea compartment that had hit the ceiling and had spilt its contents. I was lucky to remain alive and in one piece; the BMW had fulfilled its purpose, I was safe. What should have been a harrowing incident was actually the biggest meditative experience I had had. There was no tomorrow; I realised then, just then, that there was no time to waste. Then started the search – to find what was REAL.

This book is about that search and it will go back and forth with incidents, places, situations and my own experiences as I trudged the path. That search involved becoming a sanyasin, a change of name, a deep dive into many paths where I met many well-meaning teachers and also some lost souls masquerading as teachers. That quest at some point in time included practising austerities, reading some of the Holy Scriptures and engaging deeply in many a technique taught at meditation programmes. Almost everyone had a point of view of what was right, about what enabled a state of no mind. Some techniques surely provided glimpses of a timeless state. I reached a point after many years of experimenting where I realised that what I had gathered was just another load of baggage, a more refined one perhaps, but baggage nevertheless. I realised the futility of that too. This was the real accident. The earlier one was at the physical level but this one was much deeper and, what is more, I thought I was wide awake all along.

In deep surrender, I travelled to Varanasi (by train, with a one-way ticket, without an agenda), leaving everything behind. Then followed a set of magical commonplace happenings, miracles in a way, that it felt like coming home, coming home to myself. The world has never been the same since then. Food tastes better, music sounds more melodious, relationships have blossomed, sleep patterns are normal. There is a sense of deep personal freedom that allows for unlimited passion, joy and creativity in everyday life that has opened up a world of abundant possibilities across all dimensions of my life. It just feels lighter, freer and alive like never before. Sharing this magic is such a blessing.

My story, for whatever it's worth, provides just a context for the search that followed. May what I have shared serve you well. The context is actually very commonplace. It may well have been yours. There is nothing new in this book. There are no rules, no guidelines, no principles to adhere to, for there isn't any place to get to at the end that is 'out there'. There is just a rediscovery of what is already the case and all that is needed is a dropping of the baggage that hinders the seeing of that. This book then is an invitation to you to read it as a story, entertaining but also contemplative in a way, so that you can reflect on your own life and wake up from the illusion, the 'programmed state' that it is. Accepting that it is so is the first step. What allows you to realise that is your own discovery process. The rest follows as an unfolding.

Welcome to your own life. NOW.

Contents

Acknowledgements 4

Introduction 6

BOOK ONE: The Past, The Future 13

Chapter 1:

Entering the race: halfway and without choice 15

Chapter 2:

The illusion begins: frenzied and battle-ready at all times 31

Chapter 3:

Early signs of a breakdown: a blessing ahead 45

BOOK TWO: The Search, The Breakdown 59

Chapter 1:

The search: questions, books, people, processes 63

Chapter 2:

Encounters of a tantric kind: satoris, openings, possibilities 81

Chapter 3:

The real breakdown: darkness after dawn 93

Chapter 4:

The train to Varanasi: headless and in deep surrender 105

Chapter 5:

The silent vigil, grace, melody:

Manikarnika Ghat, my Teacher, the Kirtan 117

BOOK THREE: The Present, The NOW 165

Chapter 1:

Getting back to the roots 171

Chapter 2:

Letting go of the baggage 179

Chapter 3:

Including all, rejecting nothing 187

Chapter 4:

Deeply understanding, fully embracing and

transcending sexual energy 197

Chapter 5:

From rushing and grabbing to slowing down and allowing 205

Chapter 6:

Rediscovering total well-being 213

Chapter 7:

Witnessing the beginning 223

a: Walking on the edge: potential traps along the way 230

b: Writing this book: in Jaisalmer, India 236

c: Glossary of terms 238

About the author 247

BOOK ONE:
The Past, The Future

Ah This!

A moment unfolds
A story begins
A web appears
A life gets attached

Never a beginning
Never an end
Timeless, birthless
A bubble otherwise

Those awake never die
Those asleep never live
A lifetime goes by passing
A chance left aside by not waking

BOOK ONE:
The Past, The Future

Chapter 1:
Entering the race: halfway and without choice

And so life begins...

A reference gets established between 'I' and the world. First comes the name; the identification with a name that is meant to signify you, separate you from the crowd. Then come clothes, shoes, a hairstyle (with loads of hair oil if you happen to be born in India), a tribe, its prayers, its cuisine and all rituals associated with it. All is seemingly offered by whoever you live with. It is almost as if you are a doll that needs to be dressed and presented to the world. It all works well for most parts, for there is a give and take. You act the part and you get the goodies. This 'acting' is not chosen in a conscious manner as the script isn't given well in advance nor is there any formal director assisting with the entry on stage. One just has to go by the likes and dislikes of those around. It has its merits and moments of fun too. Scriptures get read, stories are told about the legacy of the family and films start to make an impact. In effect, the process of indoctrination begins without an acceptance of its validity or its authenticity. The level of dependence is so high that there's no choice anyway.

Then begins the dreaded process of schooling...

Dreaded because you are sent to school to 'learn', to 'become knowledgeable', to be 'ready' for the world. There are some schools that approach this 'get-ready-for-life' differently but I am referring to what is generally the norm. Schooling brings studies, sports, dramatics (if you are lucky) and more. Somewhere during that process, the focus, without knowing, shifts. The process is forgotten and results become important, overtly for most, covertly for some. Being better than the rest and running faster than the others are traits that get attention; perhaps 'jungle law' as articulated by humans in a civilised society, and then starts a new and distinctly uncomfortable journey. Innocence gives way to insecurity and instead of focusing on 'what is', the attention shifts to 'what might be', unconsciously, without choice. A number of questions arise, some expressed and some not but a thread of insecurity begins to take root and then starts to have a life of its own. The internal chatter that begins then, is as chaotic as it is relentless. Where will I land up in life? What will parents and teachers and society at large say about me? You could as well add to that list. The real trouble is that those ahead, parents and the like, don't have any answers. Most have opinions. Role-modelling and aping those ahead then becomes a safe option. Uniqueness then, is the first casualty. It is either watered down, shut in a time-capsule or worse still just plain uprooted. I call this period the 'lost years', when so much potential is overlooked for the mundane, for the common-place. It is almost as if the worries of the older generation are distilled into a concentrated form, much like a factory-made vanilla essence and is poured into a liquid of bliss, which then begins to take the qualities of the essence. Life is never the same again. This process of pouring in small doses or tinctures continues and the original is long forgotten. The real journey is to discover what already was perfect, before the first drop was poured in.

My life too mirrored this completely....

I was born in a small village in India and had the privilege of staying with one of the most beautiful women I have ever known, my grandmother. She was perhaps 65-66 years of age then, grey hair and a few teeth missing, but her eyes, her voice, her touch and her cooking was such that I became an early believer in the art of magic. She was just a living example of unconditional love and it was all fine while I was with her. My parents lived in Mumbai, Bombay as it was known then. We lived in one-room-kitchen chawl, a queer and unique way of defining space, but for those with a taste for geometry and 3D, the space was 180 square feet in area, that included two small rooms, a toilet and bathroom. The locality was a tough one, with ghettos peppering the landscape. The walk to and from school through some of those ghettos filled with squalor and the starkness of life then, was a sight to see. The locality was largely made up of migrants from different parts of the state and indeed the country, who had come to Mumbai in search of better prospects, their homes bare and devoid of any real luxury.

My parents were both working, which was the case then with most families in the middle to lower income bracket. My dad, from what I remember of him through the stories he recounted of his childhood and his dreams, wanted to be a cricketer and hated the life he was living, eking out a life working for the petroleum company, Shell. My mother worked in the local transportation company BEST and although we had enough on the table, life was a struggle of sorts. We had a maid to handle all matters at home when my parents were out during the day and an elder cousin sister to oversee that all was well at home. So in all there were seven of us in the small set-up, with an old and boxy Grundig radio for company that belted out some really soulful tunes in the night.

Childhood had its moments of unexplained joy when I was out of the confines of our home, spending time being with nature (climbing trees or watching birds circle the sky), with animals (adopting a stray puppy and teaching her tricks) and indulging in all things fun (kite flying, catching fish in rainwater drains and splashing through rainwater puddles). At home too, two moments clearly stood out as ones that brought everything to a standstill. The first and my favourite was my father telling me stories at bedtime after supper and the second, equally good, was being with my mother when she chanted her evening prayers by lighting a wicker lamp and singing mantras in favour of the many deities she worshipped. I wasn't interested in religion one bit. It all seemed too disconnected from reality to me even then. The sheer idea of praying and the singing, looking up to someone 'up there' who never really made contact with us, was just too silly for my liking. I had to play the game for any other option meant trouble. My father was a complete disbeliever in rituals but my mother prayed with deep devotion and a sincere intent that had the power to bring silence to the entire household, no matter what the situation was before. I liked that effect tremendously and it felt like an opportune time to begin anything new – a book or a subject to learn.

The first steps towards a 'conditioned state' began early on...

India was, and still is, a cricket-crazy nation. To top that, cricket was a passion in our household. Family get-togethers with my uncles and cousins were replete with many an informal cricketing session. Most sessions were pointless for there was surely a lack of fun and a distinct overdose of unhealthy competition, to the level of ridiculing those who lost the short cricket games that were played then. The cricketing legacy of my family began a few generations ago when my grandfather first played against an all-England team visiting unified India during the pre-partition days. My father and his brothers too had played some decent (!) level of cricket in their days but it seemed they weren't complete with that experience. That feeling of incompleteness gave rise to numerous bouts of inane and, at times, entertaining conversations about the game. A legacy was being created, verbally at least, and someone had to live up to it. Without a choice, as the eldest of the eldest, I was made the sacrificial lamb. I was marked out by all and sundry to become a cricketer. I remember having mixed feelings; partly good, for it gave me an identity in the company of my friends in school and in the locality that I grew up in, and partly of disbelief. What more can I say here? The emotions may well have been yours. So that was it then. My world as I knew it then had formed a view that I was to become a cricketer.

The other side of the coin too was being chiselled...

India loves mathematics and all things science, especially when it comes to schooling and education. It is perhaps the easiest way, other than engaging in nefarious activities, to raise one's economic status. My mother was a university top-ranker in her college days and had completed her education under the most testing of financial constraints. Her relationship with education was next to her relationship with the Divine. She would keep everything aside to ensure that her kids, me in particular, had access to the best resources for studying for my school exams. That was understandable, as the results at the end of every year and also during different times in the year brought much needed cheer within our home. There was then, a tacit understanding that I was to become an engineer, for in those days, it was but a given that boys, if they were studious, chose science and then went on to become engineers

I had two targets to aim at...a cricketer on the one hand

A cricketer and an engineer, and no one in my memory had managed such a feat (Anil Kumble, the famed Indian spinner, came much later) but who cared about all that? Just the feeling that someone in the family had dreams and aspirations to fulfil was enough joy, I suppose. Any light, feeble as it may be, in the midst of darkness is a welcome sight. My aspiration provided that and so started the process of my grounding in cricket: the visit to the grounds, 'maidans' as they were called in Mumbai; the getting up at 5:00 a.m.; the donning of whites; the hand-me-down cricket kit and more. A track was being laid. The trouble was, no one really knew the route ahead. The track was just a mile or so long, in a manner of speaking, and looked really rubbish. The horizon ahead looked daunting. It was like a game of dice or, worse still, a walk in the dark. I had to figure it out myself. That 'figuring out' process was diluted by a raft of doomsayers; fear factor, that dreaded insecurity again, external in its manifestation, was making the rounds, who said that cricket made sense if I was selected for the final eleven, at the national level! There was no IPL (the Indian Premier League) in those days and cricketers were a poor lot most of them. They ended up becoming officers in select companies that encouraged sports; a very linear route ahead or so it felt.

Then there was the role model issue about who to exemplify. A steady bat like Gavaskar or a dynamite like Vivian Richards who blasted the opposition to smithereens (I had the privilege of meeting him at a hotel gym much later and, over a glass of lemon juice, hear his life-story). Then came the question of bowling. I preferred the quicks for they looked cool and instilled fear amongst the opposition. Physiologically, I didn't have the build of a fast bowler, so a slow left-arm spin bowling option it was. Although such decisions were supposedly assisted by those in the know (!), coaches then were a disaster. I saw one chap being bribed with a gift of alphonso mangoes by a hopeful parent (my father would have none of that. Mangoes were expensive and we would rather eat one than gift it, which was another matter) and many seemed like they were waiting at a railway platform for the next train, totally disinterested in the proceedings at the nets, the platform just offering convenience. The downright asinine conversations at the nets about the technicalities of the game were too much to bear (my father and his brothers were a million times better than all the coaches that I saw) and the mental aspect of the game was totally overlooked. In the midst of all this chaos, expectations still ran high and had to be met. My father tried his best to spend time teaching me the nuances of the game but without any emotional bonding with him or with the game, you can well imagine the mental state. Still, as someone has said, 'hard work never goes to waste'. It all came to fruition: getting invited as one of the hopefuls for the Mumbai under-19 team where the stylish Sanjay Manjrekar was playing in the adjoining nets at the famed Wankhede stadium in Mumbai; captaining the engineering institute team; playing for my university; and then playing in the Surrey league for the Kingstonians.

However, the dish was never right, the ingredients always incomplete and the process a bit wayward. That was cricket then. Rather than love it as a delightful sport, which it really is, there was a world of expectations tied to the engagement and, with that, freedom was the first casualty. Imagine being a hostage to your own dreams and you will get the picture.

...and an engineer on the other

That brings us to the other significant part of the 'lost years'; education and the single-minded focus on using that as a means to uplift the socio-economic status of the family. The march from one schooling year to the next was relentless and surprisingly quick. My school was an average sort and was called AFAC (Academy of Fine Arts and Crafts, although there was nothing fine about the non-existent arts and crafts and, what is more, it was hardly an academy!) but we were blessed with a charismatic principal, a really devoted soul who tirelessly pursued his dream of making it a good institution. School memories are replete with moments of fun within the confines of our class, or at monsoon picnics with my classmates, but the inevitable question was always lurking close. What next? The question, 'What do you want to be when you grow up?' was always one to bring a deathly silence to the class; a mass of innocent souls and those with the smartest and coolest answers were always looked at with awe. I had mine: 'a cricketer', but deep down I had no conviction within about being one. Still, it managed to give me some space and identity amongst a 'sea of sperms', as one of my closest pals described the bunch. India loves engineers and doctors. So many are churned out every year and at some subliminal level, it was decided that I had to become one. I wasn't the best at mathematics or science (although a good teacher can make all the difference in the way a subject is accessed and we had a distinctly 'tired' bunch of teachers at school, save a few) and had to 'keep at it' for want of any other alternative. Growing up in a crowded locality, a melting pot of sorts and in a family strained by economic and emotional tensions (which I realised later were commonplace) was an experience of sorts, a rapid progress to maturity as some would say.

A crisis of sorts was brewing and a 'growing up' ahead of time was but natural...

Life trudged along and the landscape then was just a mix of sporadic attention to studies, cricket and an emotional awkwardness that was perhaps common to almost all those who were in the same league as I was in. The tension at home, brought upon by a variety of factors starting first with a mismatched chemistry between my parents, their own frustrations about the life they were living and a distinct lack of financial certainty (the piggy bank was the saviour in the last week of every month) was such that I did not want to add to their woes by bringing any of my 'stuff' into the pot. Lack of chemistry between molecules implies inertness or volatility or both and that was how it was at home then; inertness in the main but extreme volatility during certain conditions, brought upon by even the slightest changes to the *status quo*. At moments when some of my stuff did fall in by chance, the decibel levels at home and the silence that followed soon after were both at such extremes that it started to resemble some of the films I remember seeing then. Life imitating art or the other way round was an early experience. It was during such times that two incidents created a huge pain and shame within me that they perhaps altered very much how I related to life and to people in my life after that. Understanding 'cause and effect' or the 'karma' theory was too early a time then.

Innocence lost...a watchful eye from then on

'Sexual abuse' as a term is potent with so many nuances for those who read it as a subject of interest, but for those who actually experience it in their childhood, life takes an added and a totally different dimension to its unfolding. I had two such incidents between the ages of five and nine. We had a maid who was to take care of me during the day when I was perhaps five years of age, and also support my mother with any household work that needed attention in the evening.

The daily routine was a fixed one in that I was with her after my school time, until my aunt, who was also staying with us, came home from her college. I won't go into what happened by way of the ongoing sexual abuse from the maid that continued for about two years, other than the fact that it just felt weird to be in the company of anyone older than me after that. The other incident happened during one of the festivals in India called 'Kojagiri'. This is a harvest festival, celebrated on the full moon day between the months of September and October. It celebrates the ending of the rainy season and the welcoming of the harvest period that is to follow later. An all-night vigil is observed and the goddess of wealth is worshipped for inviting greater prosperity in the lives of those who worship her. As can be expected, any such opportunity is used by children to just have a good time and an all-night vigil; that too, supported by parents, is just the stuff to allow for unbridled fun. I was about nine or ten and was on our building terrace at night when I was approached by an older boy who was perhaps 20-21 himself and was invited to accompany him to the quiet corners of the terrace. It all seemed harmless and without any malicious intent till it became clear that he just wanted to 'jerk' himself off and needed me to just 'sit' on his lap. All this happened as the terrace was filled with another 20 to 25 boys of different age groups; the shame of having had to go through such an ordeal was something I could not deal with, let alone speak to anyone about. It just ensured that I retreated quietly into my 'shell' and remained tight-lipped about the reasons for doing so. I also made a mental note to become stronger in the future, to 'straighten out' those who dominated me. Little did I know that that attitude ensured I related to any issue to do with dominance or disagreement from a deeply primal level.

A shock absorber for the frustrations of the immediate world... accepting without a murmur

There is, as I know now, an almost programmed tendency within many to just pass their frustrations on to those who can't respond back. The weak, the innocent and those who can't speak back then, in turn, become 'shock absorbers' in such cases. That explains perhaps why in spite of the abundance that is so evident in life, there is so much exploitation in the world we live in. My life too had its share of such moments when I was a silent and an unwilling 'shock absorber' to those who I knew to be close relatives of mine. Our lack of a firm financial footing as a family ensured that those who were around had some form of 'positional' superiority over me and then followed a seemingly mindless and at times unpardonable set of behaviours (verbal abuse, physical violence) from those who were senior. Given that my parents were already mired in their own 'life-soup', I just kept it all to myself, reinforcing the fact that I felt I needed to take care of myself. Two incidents stand out for the sheer callous manner in which those who were meant to be responsible acted out their frustrations.

I was about twelve years of age, visiting my grandmother, and was enjoying the quiet time in the peaceful setting that was her home. My uncle, my dad's younger brother, had just quit his job and was going through a personal crisis at that time. He had taken to the bottle and the early signs of an alcoholic life were becoming clear. It was on one of the evenings when my grandmother was out shopping for the household that he asked me to visit the local arrack shop to purchase some country liquor (house wine isn't the same as country liquor). The experience of walking into a shop that was at one end of the town, the sight of a hundred drunken eyes staring back at me and then me mustering the courage to ask for the required brew, was one that caused an instant 'growing up'. The shame, the fear and the shock of being alone in a cesspool of sorts with the dregs of society, as I saw them then, was just too much for my mind to handle. It just blanked out to allow for a glassy stare from my eyes that perhaps allowed for a natural desensitisation of the moment. I was short in height and the cash counter was so tall that even if I stood on my toes, I was still a good six inches short of the edge. The guy selling the stuff looked over the counter and looked down at me, laughed his guts off and then proceeded to fill a pint of the local brew in a bottle that was just washed and kept dry. He then asked me to stuff the bottle in my pants, lest the local cops single me out for attention. That done, I left the shop and stopped as instructed to pick up some spicy snacks for my uncle and handed over the goods to him and his friend. My grandmother was livid when she heard this and ensured that I was never left alone at home but the mental conditioning within had set by then; I was determined to protect myself and also 'teach' such toughies a lesson.

The other incident happened when I was about thirteen when I was in Mumbai. One of my uncles had come to stay with us for a while and on Monday morning, after my parents had left for work, he made his way out to meet someone in the city. This was right in the midst of summer holidays and I was at home, doing nothing in particular but waiting for some silence to descend. It was then that he just barged back into our home and demanded his wallet! I was taken aback by his demand and mentioned that I had nothing to do with what was missing but he was on some rage that he just could not handle. Then began a brutal and inhuman physical violence that stayed the course for an hour or so till he got tired from sheer exhaustion. It then dawned on him to search the area where he had hung his trousers for the night and there, under the cupboard, was his wallet, untouched and covered in a bit of dust. Without looking directly at me and without a word of apology, he left our home and that was the end of the matter, as far as everyone else was concerned. While there was a family that I was a part of, I just felt like an orphan, having to fend for myself.

We stayed in a tough locality; a dozen or so government-owned tenements that were surrounded by huts (immigrants from all parts of India) and there was an almost everyday occurrence of violence, domestic or otherwise, across the area. I was instructed by my father not to mix with any of the kids staying in that locality (his reasons were perfectly legitimate, as he feared that I'd pick up some of the habits and traits of those in the vicinity) but that led to an untenable situation for me. I was the 'lone wolf' in the locality and the alpha male in each group that I kept away from ensured that I was under constant surveillance and threat. There was many an occasion where I had to deal with physical violence and a group one at that, that I had to endure and the saying 'what can't kill you can only make you stronger' started to make sense at an early age. I was keeping all of what was happening outside of the confines of our home to myself and the only point of conversation between me and my parents was about my studies and the good results that followed regularly.

A real trouble-maker at school...a real nightmare for teachers

That brings me to school, which in a surreal way provided the only real outlet for my emotional and mental angst. My classmates were a lovely bunch; innocent faces who I shared so many years with who became my extended family for the ten years that we shared together. School became a place for me to just express myself totally; dramatics, sports (whatever little the school could afford), excursions and studies. As long as the academic results were good (average plus and my ranking in the class within single digits), all was tolerated. My class register was perpetually filled with remarks from class teachers, each one complaining about my 'troublesome' behaviour (making my classmates laugh was my favourite pastime and taking on some of the tough teachers, something I felt naturally compelled to). Some went so far as to suggest that I be expelled from school or sent to a boarding school where the disciplinary standards were rumoured to be far tougher.

The constant emotional and physical violence at home was a regular feature and I felt like a caged animal would perhaps, just as it's captured from the wild. There were many times I considered running away from home (another influence of the films in those days) but stopped short of acting on it for the trouble it would cause to those who loved me. The pain and shame that I was carrying inside, though, seemed like a ghost that would take control without warning, leading to many situations that I found myself in for which I had no explanation. The one incident that I remember was about setting off a fire in our kitchen at home one Sunday morning when my parents were asleep. The kitchen curtain was ablaze and an orange glow was visible from the drawing room. My father rushed in to douse the flames that had by then spread across the length of the kitchen window, just in time to stop it from touching the gas cylinder in our home.

A fire was burning within, though, and I would imagine that emotional maturity that comes with biological growth becomes a non-starter in such situations, for the focus is just on survival. Like the many millions who suffer silently, I presume I too was in that space – growing up but without a clue of how to connect with the world, how to be open and how to listen to someone's heart because, for that, the one pre-requisite is an open heart in the first place. Mine was long shut.

That is how it felt.

BOOK ONE:
The Past, The Future

Chapter 2:
The illusion begins: frenzied and battle-ready at all times

The march was relentless...the desire to control the next moment, day, month, year and more

After school came junior college and the results indicated that I was 'in the middle', a common experience for most people I suppose later on in life but that is how it felt. I had neither made it to the best engineering colleges nor were the results so bad that I could be labelled a 'dumbo'. To make matters worse, an astrologer friend of the family, an old chap who apparently 'read out' the 'futures' of many a politician (I came to know later when attending business school that the word meant something else, but both were shots in the dark and both equally vague) had written down his take on what the future had in store for me. He had said that I would drop out of school and be a part of a local mafia by the time I was eighteen (Bollywood was replete those days, with films that had such 'masala' plots and perhaps the poor soul had had an overdose of a few such films). That was a crucial moment at home. My mother, steadfast as she was in the midst of the damnedest of storms, was in a brooding and worrisome state; the oracle had spoken apparently. My father, the cricketer in him refused to buckle down to a stupid umpiring decision (how could a batsman be declared out before he took to the crease?) cared two hoots to say the least and was quiet in his expression. That is how the situation was and this was just before the crucial exams (the Indian version of the 'A' levels) were to commence. The timing couldn't have been more 'opportune'.

I made a decision then to write down my future at that very moment (all the dreams that, when fulfilled, would make us all happy). I wrote that down on the adjoining page next to the very one on which the astrologer had written his version of the Bollywood script. I then tore off his page and chewed it with relish. Paper never tasted so delicious (that is another twist to the Bollywood script 'The kid writes his own future'). I am laughing my guts off now at the ridiculousness of the whole episode but back then, I kid you not, the background score was playing (*Rocky* was not released then but *The Eye of the Tiger* would have been perfect), temple bells were ringing and it just felt good for no reason. So then began a definitive state, driven by what was on paper, that saw me through the IIT entrance (one of the most competitive exams within India for those wanting to study engineering) and then later the IIMs (one of the best of the business schools in India) and then to London to a firm that was regarded as an icon in its class, Goldman Sachs. 'Luck favours the prepared mind', is what I had read on the desk of a wizard at KPMG but I must say that joining the firm Goldman Sachs, where the people were referred to as 'Masters of the Universe' was largely due to the efforts and the goodwill of some really creative and talented souls from KPMG and I am grateful to them for that privilege. Life at Goldman Sachs deserves a separate section and I will come to that later in this book.

Engineering studies at IT BHU at Varanasi (Varanasi is also known as Kashi or Benares) was a nightmare of sorts. Those in search of 'spiritual solace' head to Varanasi and it is still quite popular on the 'meaning of life' seekers circuit, but for me at that age, seventeen, it was like a prison sentence. Six subjects every term and eight terms to go through; that sounded and felt like a lot of paper to go through and chewing it would not help. The batch was a motley bunch, representing India in every way; almost every state and economic section of India seemed to be represented. I could well write a whole book about the four years at Varanasi but a young and talented Indian author by the name of Chetan Bhagat came out with his version about life in the IITs that was then made into a very successful film in India. I bet that if a vote was taken, a BHU book would be in its own class, a place where religion, politics, student life and a general state of anarchy all combined to form a deliciously homogenous mix, 'Banaras-style', that I could only label as truly Indian. The perpetual worry about the 'what next?' question seemed to make its presence felt even at BHU, as our final exams lurked close and most had a job offer on hand. I hated the thought of sitting behind a computer and punching at the keys and creating some software program for use in some application. The first aspect that made that 'hate' even more stark was that I did not have the aptitude for software programming (I did get an offer that needed me to sign some 'bond' and that killed the possibility immediately) and the second was that I loved the sun and the sky so much that I would rather sit under a tree than in an air-conditioned office.

Let me cut to the near-past so that we move ahead. I was 'living the life' in London (in the eyes of those close to me, at least, that was what it felt like) but I wasn't sure this was all there was to life. Getting married, parenting and all the lovely moments that come with it were present in abundance, the bank balance looked healthy (for a guy who had started out in a chawl in Mumbai all this was unbelievable) and the future seemed predictable. The fire within was raging though, in a manner of speaking, for deeper questions were still unresolved. London, and the West in general, is a very organised place and that helped get the curtains and the bedcovers in the right form and in the right colour; the façade was just perfect and fine but the core was totally unstable.

The pressures at work, especially at Goldman Sachs, were distinctly being felt as life was being mortgaged to some future ideal state (kids in good schools, a home with a garden and a few cars parked outside and all the trappings that came with it). The trouble was, this seemingly ideal state wasn't one that

I had crafted on my own, out of my own free choice. Everyone seemed to be on the same treadmill, the same dreams or illusions if you will and evening and weekend conversations in the social circles of those days were so plain boring – almost devoid of life. Not many were really present to the moment and instead of being human, open and sensitive, in its place was a bunch of men and women wearing masks and speaking banalities. To add to that, my health was suffering. To placate the hunger or to douse the fire, the initial search was filled with the usual 'quick fix' approaches by reading 'self-help' books and the like, as well as attending short courses that offered meditation as a means to deal with the mess that was apparent.

An allopathic approach has its merits for it douses the symptoms with so many chemicals that the body just forgets the cause, the original reason for the discomfort, and deals with the new effects of the altered bio-chemistry. Some lousy trick this, for the underlying discomfort deep down remains, in a dormant and suppressed state, to make its presence felt later, directly or indirectly, in some form of physical or mental manifestation. My state was like that, given the degrees of freedom available to me and my own 'waking' state or lack of it.

The trappings at work and the seemingly 'perfect' lifestyle was a big draw and there was always the evening or weekend 'drink-eat-socialise-see a film' combination to dull the senses. Having a family also provided a balm of sorts in many a physical and emotional way but in moments of silent contemplation, the noise within, the angst rather, was unbearable. I remember a time one early spring morning when I looked in the mirror in our bathroom and was shocked and dispirited to see what I was seeing in front of me. The eyes looked tired, the skin a bit puffed up, the energy levels at a new low; a 'Dorian Gray' moment perhaps, as he sees his real image and then stabs his own picture on the wall in disgust and then starts to see the underlying reality come to the surface. It was an unbelievable moment, a longish one, for I stood still looking at the mirror and, in the same instant, also heard a younger, innocent voice (my memories of my childhood coming alive in one inspiring spark) reach out by wanting to break free from the shackles of the 'reality' that was. Goldman Sachs was one massive part of that reality and so now is an opportune time to share the mystery that is the firm and the magic and the muddle that it created in my life.

Life at Goldman Sachs was an eye-opener, a play of extremes... absolutely great in parts and downright stressful in others

Goldman Sachs is a firm in preparation for war. Everything is visualised and planned to the last detail and then executed with ruthless precision. Losing is a feeling that the firm does not like and yet it plays the game (war) in the most ethical way (as far as I know, the recent financial meltdown notwithstanding). The firm's emphasis on selecting the best, training them to be super-efficient at chosen tasks, making them battle-ready for the trickiest situations and engendering a feeling of being a part of a bigger team, is an experience to go through. They are good, really super-good at that.

Goldman's brought global travel, enabled working in diverse markets ranging from China to Australia, the US and Europe and all in between. The access to the best in the best of firms was at a scale that was unprecedented. The risks were high and so were the rewards. The stakes were big as were the revenue targets at the firm level and the mobilisation effort to get battle-ready was at a scale I was not used to. The firm managed to do all this in an almost 'normal' fashion without breaking into any sweat and that was an amazing process to experience. The systems laid down at the firm allowed for unbelievable consistency and technology and its smart use and meant that the firm never slept; some part of its global operation was always awake, from Tokyo to London to San Francisco and all the others in between. Telecommunications and use of the internet and smartphones gave me then, way back in 2000, a first-hand feel of what it meant to be 'always on', 24/7. Some of the senior partners in the firm looked and behaved like Hollywood actors but the difference was that they had their own scripts and did a far better job than the ones on the screen. All this was great and it made one feel part of a bigger entity, a rapidly marching and seemingly invincible army that knew no fear and had planned to the last detail and yet was totally flexible to the demands of the battlefield. It was an experience to go through and Goldman Sachs as a firm, as I see it now, was just the best at constantly perfecting the art of enabling capital mobility, seeing capital as liquid, which in turn allowed for a flow of its own accord.

Life is sight and sound show for most. What is seen and how something is heard determines its receptivity with those who listen. The race to the top for the best assignments, for the highest bonuses and more, was a 24/7 one, much in the background but very much active in sentiment. The first criteria was whether one looked the part and acted the stuff well; being a part of the pack and so the need to fit in, was at a subliminal level, almost a given. Whether it was at KPMG earlier or at Goldman Sachs later, consistency mattered and that trait was carried through across everything to do with work, attire included. When I first arrived in the UK to join KPMG in 1999, I noticed that the reception or better still, the acceptance within the firm was mixed. Overtly, all seemed well and there was always the growth opportunity that was available to target. Meanwhile, the undercurrent, much in the unsaid, was one of being perceived as an outsider and my clothes became the first thing to be noticed. Both KMPG and Goldman Sachs are top-class firms with the best of human resource policies but what I am saying was energetically expressed; subliminal footprints them all. The feedback I received from a 6ft 3in half-Swedish, half-Spanish blonde colleague was that, while all was well with the intellectual rigour with which I participated, my overall get-up wasn't hacking it within the firm. The attire and the overall look 'n' feel, I felt then, came in the way of the dream that was being lived and so corrective action was in order. Her advice to me was that I spend my way out of the state I was in, invest in myself at a level I had not done before. She was associated with recruitment activities for KPMG in those days and was to head to Milan to interview hopefuls from one of the leading business schools in that city. I was invited to be a part of the team that visited the campus on a Friday afternoon. Over the next two days and with a good GBP5000 or so spent, I came back with a new haircut and a new wardrobe that included a few suits, shirts, ties and shoes. The experience over the next few days and then later was immediately discernible in that the shift from a 'resource pool' team member to a frontline lead on assignments happened without effort. Nothing truly had changed within but much had changed on the surface (although that did have an impact on how I felt) and that was enough for the shift to occur. The subliminal power of the senses and their role in decisions became evident like never before.

Another experience at Goldman Sachs made that clear and I was amazed at how important such small things were in the larger scheme of things at work. I was in my second year at the firm and was given feedback by my mentor at the firm (bless the Frenchman) that my accent wasn't helping my progress within the firm. Then started the process of meeting many a voice training expert that finally led me to a West End drama school that practised its arts in North London every Saturday, where I enrolled as a member. What followed over a period of 18 months was an experience of a lifetime as I was in the midst of stage and film hopefuls, lovely souls who had just one dream, that of making it big on the stage or celluloid. The sheer emphasis on diction and delivery was so high that my own vocal range started to expand and settle into its own. Years later, as a part of my search I met an 87-year-old Kiwi actor at one of the many meditation retreats that I was attending who suggested a very simple beginning to any conversation or speech. She was an ex-BBC actor and a Master in her own right, meditative in every way and suggested that I deeply feel the emotion first of what I was saying and just stay there while sharing what I had to share. That altered the opportunity landscape that I was seeing ahead and it was clear that the sight and sound show together was making a huge difference.

The world of opportunities and sensory experiences just expanded geometrically soon after, as I travelled the globe from the USA to China and almost every other country that mattered in between. Cities such as Sydney, San Francisco, Shanghai or Seoul became places to fly into for meetings and then leave in a few days. The quality of the meetings, the scope of the conversations and the possibilities ahead all made for a heady mix and the dream was being lived well, or so I thought. In particular, the stay at the Ritz Carlton in New York in a room overlooking the Hudson Bay and the Statue of Liberty was a long one; over a year with weekend trips back to London. The sheer ease of sampling the simplest and perhaps the subtlest of cuisines was also a heady experience, as the local chefs in many of the hotels across the world where I stayed started to provide an 'off the menu list' option to a now familiar face.

CEOs are a lonely bunch and their insecurity with their position meant that anyone who gave them the best advice to stay the course and win would get their attention and win their business. Goldman Sachs was and is perhaps the best in its league and that 'mindset' percolated right down to the new recruits in the firm. The relentless search for the next best, the most latest, all driven by the need for survival which, in turn, was fuelled by the stock markets which backed 'winners', meant that there was no real rest; the conversations with leading companies and their leadership teams was an ongoing process.

The guys I worked with made for an interesting bunch; creative to the core, relentless in their march but they seemed too serious for their own good. The illusion was just too overwhelming that they refused to see anything else. 'Creativity within defined limits' or 'within the narrow confines of a PowerPoint slide' was the norm and, as can be expected, the burn-out rate was high and so it continued and perhaps still does. There surely was and still is an overdose of masculine energy in such environments; targets, achievement, winning and then back again to setting new targets, within the firm and indeed the industry. Silent witnessing and a return to simplicity are unheard of in that industry. They'd see that as a sign of impending lunacy. "Tree huggers are a queer lot" is how one banker expressed it then and that comment perhaps sums it all up.

Holidays every year to exotic destinations and more were like a perk that was to be tasted but the return to the treadmill was inevitable. The family seemed happy, the in-laws and parents content that 'all was well' and that the 'dream' was being lived to its fullest potential. Any questions that challenged the *status quo* or the very assumptions of life were looked at with suspicion by those around for they were all in the same boat: living their lives but without questioning its direction. No one really had any view on some of the deeper questions that were on my mind or rather in my heart. The general refrain from those close to me, well-meaning as they were in their intentions, ranged from the mildly lukewarm to the plain cold or the downright silly. Statements such as 'this isn't a quest for householders' or 'take a holiday to Mauritius...it's breath-taking' or 'only a Buddha can answer these questions...no one else' were those that made the rounds and I stopped conversations with those around me altogether. I was upsetting their boat in a way, altering their state of reality by my questioning and it did not seem fair on them.

The dreams I was living, the external expression of success, were all fine but they, at some silent level, really made no difference to me. I was happy that my kids were in good schools and that all seemed well from a material stand-point but the feeling after all that was one of leaving a stadium as a spectator. I was feeling that I wasn't participating 100% in my life and that what was important to me was of no consequence to the world. The game had to be played. This is what I suppose the term 'work-life balance' alludes to and mine seemed totally out of kilter. So then what could one do but stick with the tried and tested? I then created an even bigger illusion to live out: that of starting my own company and seeing it grow. The idea then was to use innovation, energy and the network of contacts to stay 'ahead of the game' and make enough money so that I could 'retire early' and then pursue what was important to me. That seemed like a task and a half and one surely to keep me occupied, or rather pre-occupied, and away from thinking of the 'road less travelled'.

Faster, higher, better...an illusion at its peak

Managing money after an investment banking career was the obvious choice and so it was; another track was set, a faster one at that. It kind of also seemed normal to take that step as I had just turned 40 and the 'network', the terse and rather insipid term used to define the contacts that one has in the business world, was alive and active. I term this as the 'illusion at its peak' for it's a big and bold bet and if that bet turns out tops, there are riches at the end, a castle perhaps. A small mistake and a nightmare begins; maya in reverse!

I raised capital to invest in Indian real estate, a sector that showed promise but was known to be thoroughly corrupt in its workings. It had archaic laws and a million loopholes and many more rabbit holes where cash could disappear overnight, and yet some of the richest in the land had their origins in real estate. So there I was – capital, goodwill and an open territory. I was running a business that was set up with investors (three very wise souls from the USA and a big firm in the UK, whose CEO was a large-hearted man and the Chairman, a visionary in his own right).

The game was tough, bloody and at times without rules. Books talk about setting rules to win. This was like playing a game of poker and I just wasn't up for it. From farmers to land sharks to brokers to real estate developers and then the financiers, all driven by greed and fear, were swimming the waters in search of their next meal and also saving their skins. The big fish had a field day while the small fry made do by siding up with the big ones, partaking of the leftovers. The complex web of intricate relationships, archaic laws and a rapidly growing economy 'aided' by a corrupt bureaucracy ensured almost perfect conditions for a mini gold-rush of sorts and a feeding frenzy was but a given. It was heady at times but the underlying current had greed and fear as the main drivers. The extent of personal compromise was just too much for me to commit to. The first year of the set-up was a near-blank one and the second did see a few transactions but the battle was over; the end seemed in sight. One of the UK firms that I was dealing with decided to pull out of India as the market by then had shifted to negative. In spite of all efforts to revive their position, there wasn't much that was possible and they quit their India plans. That was an emotional low for me as I was hoping they would last the distance and taste success but it just wasn't meant to be. I had reached a place alien to me. The wheels had got stuck, the fuel was fast running out and I did not like the view of where I was and how the landscape looked ahead.

The candle burning at both ends...a double life lived to its extreme

I was, right from my business school days in the early 1990s, searching for lasting peace, one that was not dependent on achievement; the treadmill mindset was just too one-dimensional. That search, however, was part-time by way of effort. The quest to transcend the cycle of fulfilment and suffering was always a real one and an uncomfortable one too. The suffering seemed endless, as the baggage of memories seemed heavy and the sheer futility of the moments of short-lived happiness brought on by small worldly achievements, too ridiculous to take attention away and then live in a semi-comatose state. Prayers taught at home as a child did not help and visits to temples seemed futile (they seemed like a circus, with loads of rituals and a host of middlemen interpreting the experience) and chats with friends and elders, as I mentioned earlier, proved inconclusive. None inspired confidence that there was some light to be found. So a double life was being lived, as do the silent minority living in the world, where I was seeking my own truth and also competing for attention and capital in the world. Some state that was, for at one point in time I just could not identify with who I was becoming. The child-like innocence, the zest for life, the free and daring spirit, the spark in things mundane – all those seemed missing, dormant perhaps, and surely not in action.

Birth, conditioning and a conditioned life full of dogmas, beliefs and rituals and then finally death; this is how life was. There was no real truth that was experienced; one that was based on a personal knowing but in its place was but a baggage of ready reckoners or a ready reference guide to cross-check what showed up. How could I be alive, truly alive? Most have an inbuilt guide-book, accessed almost unconsciously, and live out programmes that short-circuit the gap to ensure that the uncertainty or the unknown isn't experienced. The discovery of the state before the identification with form and all that comes with it was a discovery worth making.

A real investigation was warranted. That is how it felt.

BOOK ONE:
The Past, The Future

Chapter 3:
Early signs of a breakdown: a blessing ahead

From mild fevers and colds to stubborn illnesses...the drop was real

The vehicle was holding fine so far. There were signs that it was creaking at the edges and needing an overhaul. Sleep patterns were becoming a bit erratic and the occasional social drink in the evening gave way to an almost regular 'glass of red wine' experience. That seemed normal as the wine aided the slow drift into sleep. The worrying part was the mornings never felt like they did before. A cup of strong tea or coffee was the only way to fire up the sleeping tamasic animal that the body-mind had become. This too seemed normal behaviour for it was socially acceptable and commonplace but I was hating the increasing dependency on such stimulants first thing in the morning and then throughout the day. Most in the 40 years and more range seemed destined to this slow walk as did the seemingly irreversible shift in weight patterns and waist sizes. Although I was in no way overweight, let alone obese, there surely was a feeling that my health was slowly getting out of control.

Work pressures meant that any small fever or cold had to be quickly doused so that one could function back at work. I started to notice a particular pattern of illness that made my body its host at specific times in the year. At the onset of spring in London and later in the year at the onset of autumn, my throat used to stop functioning for a good seven to fourteen days. After a million antibiotic courses and a few tests, I was told it was laryngitis that I was suffering from. It seemed then that I was destined to live this misery; that is how the doctors made it out to be. The other niggle that became a nightmare started with my lower back and then spread to the whole body. What was earlier in my late 30s a slight pain in the lower back and then the whole body, that could be dealt with by a hot bath or a monthly trip to a good spa, was now a regular all-nighter. That was when I was recommended painkillers, for the source of the problem could not be diagnosed. As is the customary wont of our times, a shotgun approach, in effect the use of painkillers, did allay the symptoms but I was now experiencing greater acidity in my system and the taste buds were only picking up flavours in the ultra ranges; subtlety was the first casualty.

To make matters worse I had started to smoke, occasionally to begin with but later one to two cigarette packs a day. The smell of tobacco on my clothes, the odd hue of my skin from the tar that was inhaled and the slight nicotine stain on the back of my teeth meant that social overtones at home against the habit started to get stronger. My clothes started being kept and washed separately and my kids refused to give the absolutely wonderful 'welcome home' hug. The lowest point of that state was a gift given to me by my daughter; a six-page essay on the irrefutable link between cancer and smoking. Most self-help books spoke of the inextricable link between the body and mind and that almost all (I would go to the extent of saying all, given what I know now) diseases were psychosomatic in nature, most beginning with some mental affliction. If all that were true, then the condition of my body said many a thing about the state of my mind and that did not make for good listening.

I responded to all these bodily complaints by trying to get it into better shape through exercise and the like, but without a real change in lifestyle and diet there wasn't much that was possible. The only comfort then was that I looked and appeared much younger than most of my contemporaries; a shallow compensation but still a really sorry state of affairs.

A drop in attention span...signs of an impending fatigue

I was also noticing that my attention span during meetings and over telephone calls was coming down to abysmal levels. A strong coffee and some sugar acted as a booster; that became the first middle-age addiction, in a manner of speaking. The odd 10km run in Richmond Park in London, a trek in one of the mountain ranges in India, the membership of a gym, the buying of new pair of ASICS running shoes and a bicycle to match, the practice of yoga and pranayam or the attending of short meditation courses helped but were limited in their impact.

As someone leading a business to growth, I had many a responsibility but the body was tired and the mind fatigued. The demands of the business were 24/7 and the usual canvas of life then included loads of air travel (to India and the USA from my home in London), a constant review of financial opportunities, of term sheets, shareholder agreements, land record contracts, collections and payments and more. I had a small but trustworthy and capable team in India (two lovely souls Abhishek and Tapas who gave their best) but my own single-minded attention was missing. This, I contemplated then, wasn't one out of physical lethargy, boredom or a lack of intellectual horsepower but for the main reason that I wasn't sure what my life was meant to signify. I was tired of the self-created circus that I was a part of and there was no other option in sight. The investors who had backed me and my plans were very supportive and understood the challenges that the Indian market presented but the real challenge that I was faced with was far, far darker. I was crumbling within when all seemed perfect on the outside. The burden of their expectations and the responsibility of handling their money was a big one to bear and that too had its impact in making the entire structure even more untenable.

Relationships becoming distant...a disconnect with emotions

Close relationships were becoming distant and the factory of desires was churning out newer and newer designs; the combined spectacle was a sight to see. Some call it a mid-life crisis while others term it a mid-life waking up but from site 'ground-zero', it felt like a crisis in every way. Along the way some really beautiful souls showed up, opening up a world of meaningful, gentle and at times hilarious conversations that brought some respite but the darkness within, or perhaps the shadow of the past, was getting bigger and bigger in its footprint. There was hope that the state would change, although I now see 'hope' as such a terrible word, for 'living in hope' implies missing the NOW completely.

My relationship with my parents, sisters and wife started to suffer as I remained quiet about what was going on in my life and carried on with the 'act' that provided the illusory certainty between us. Conversations with close friends whom I had known for over two or three decades were becoming mundane and I realised that I was creating this experience through the mechanics of my mind. My kids were very young then, four and nine years of age, and they provided the much-needed joy and celebration to an increasingly isolated mind. A visit to a counsellor or a psychotherapist was not of much help as the theory was clear in my head and I had read much of what was relevant. I was really at a stage of experimenting with various meditative techniques and checking their validity in addressing the symptoms that were so apparent in my life. I was keeping a diary; a log of things to do, to break out of the limiting state I was in and had set a timeframe for its roll-out. The trouble was, I did not know what good looked like as the past did not provide any clues and those in the near vicinity, people I knew, did not inspire confidence or provide any references.

Then the unexpected....a blessing

And then the biggest blessing (as I look back at it now) in a long, long time happened. I was travelling home after a two-day meditation programme organised in the British countryside somewhere in Dorset and was tired from a multitude of factors, jet lag being the least of them although I did realise that I wasn't sleeping too well during normal sleeping hours. The time was 1:20 a.m. and I was on the M3 which is a straight road, an expressway, to London. Somewhere along the way, as I started to feel sleepy, I stopped at a service station at a Costa's outlet to pick up a cup of black tea and a snack. I left immediately after that and was on the M3, a straight road to the city. The expressway was relatively quiet at this time, cars and the occasional truck driving at a speed that looked faster than normal. My eyes were closing and I was going in and out of the normal waking state now and then. That too was a nice experience and I had the trust that I would manage to remain awake and on the straight. This thinking and acting worked well until I was on the M3. The road crossed the M25, a ring road that circles London and is a busy one during the day. This road too was quiet and it seemed normal to just push along at the suggested maximum speed and so there I was, just inching faster to get home and to see off another day. There were thoughts about tomorrow, thoughts about all sorts of silly matters ranging from the wisdom of taking a shower at home after arriving to eating a bowl of oats, honey and rice milk. There were others too, but my reaching out to the tea compartment for a sip broke the chain for some others, random them all, to follow.

Travelling at 70 miles an hour at midnight, tired and sleepy, can be lethal and so it was. I don't know what happened just before but I may have slept for a fraction longer than normal and heard a big bang. It woke me out of my tired and sleepy state in an instant, the same moment and the body was on 'high alert' immediately. The mind too, for a long and extended period for the first real time, was also on alert, watching what was happening. I could smell gunpowder, nitrogen charge I was told later that sets off the air-bags, and also had the feel of glass on my face and neck. The temperature had suddenly dropped as the cool night air was flowing through the smashed glass window. The hazard lights had come on and the car was still at some speed, struggling to find a way to distance itself from the steel and concrete barrier in the middle. This is when the car took a small left turn, no real doing by me at this stage, at least consciously, and I realised that there was no way to accelerate as the car controls had taken over. It was then that I saw a huge trailer, a goods-laden, some 16-wheel truck, behind me as my car was cutting lanes to head to the hard shoulder on the left. There really was nothing I could do but watch, just watch. It was all so clear as I saw white powder coming out of the trailer's wheels as it braked hard to avoid a collision. The honk from the trailer sounded melodious and similar to the ones I used to hear as a child when diesel goods trains used to pass our village at night.

This was amazing, the entire experience. It all seemed liked a lifetime and I just saw my whole life pass by; from the little boy who flew kites, who played with dogs, who climbed trees, who was hurt and ridiculed, to the teenager who put the effort to create breakthroughs to the young adult wanting to make it big in life, to finally the people I had hurt to then my loved ones and then a full stop. What should have been a harrowing experience was actually the biggest blessing I had ever received. Rather than get agitated at the loss of my car and the hassle of being stuck on a highway at midnight, the heartbeat felt normal, more normal than normal really. In just an instant I saw and realised the baggage I was carrying in my life, in all areas of my life, and realised the mechanics of the mind as it postponed, compared and judged to delay the truth of the moment. The quality of silence was of a very different kind immediately after the accident as I felt a huge distance between me and my thoughts, between me and my body. I can't describe it any better than this but I felt that I was neither the body nor the mind and, in that state, there were no worries but just a stillness that did not need to be still to be still. Its very nature was one of silent celebration. Ah! The intoxication of that extended period, those set of moments, was unbelievable and a lasting experience, not to be forgotten by anything, really. Time seemed to stop still. I was hooked for sure and did not know what to say to anyone. There was just gratitude that I was alive and it must have been the blessings of those around in my life and before that I survived the mishap.

A highway patrol car made its way to the site and the two officers in typical British humour remarked that I was lucky to have remained in one piece. I remember one of them saying that in the fight between the car and the road divider, the latter always wins. The air was crisp cold and the sound of the occasional car passing by was not a distraction at all. Everything felt seamless, in unison, as the division-creating mind was at rest; time had ceased to be important at all. The experience of the NOW was real and I realised that the addiction to the word 'tomorrow' was actually a disease for it really did not exist. Those few moments during the accident and the silent forty minute ride back home seemed like an eternity. There was no tomorrow; there really was no tomorrow to postpone stuff to. I mean, who wanted to come back again and wander aimlessly in search of the elusive state of peace when it seemed all available for free, in an instant?

Life felt half-lived and the accident brought a number of things to the surface. For one, instead of a traumatic experience and possible expensive post-accident therapy, I was actually feeling much better. The second was about facing up to the sheer vulnerability of life. Some of my close friends and business partners suggested I redouble my efforts at work. I was already at quadruple levels, so a doubling meant working at an eight-fold capacity; the only way I was going to make that happen was if I took to steroids! It did feel very calm though. The sheer blank state during the accident was like a satori of the highest order where everything seemed perfect as it was, immensely beautiful; shattered glass, the smell of gunpowder, the flashing hazard lights and the powder coming off the wheel of the 16-wheel trailer and life unfolding, including everything. There was no running away but just witnessing what was; extremely hypnotic in every way. I could hear my heart beat then, feel my breath and it felt just so expansive and, for that brief but extended period, life seemed perfect. There was no baggage to handle, no issues to deal with and my story did not exist.

Coming back to the earlier 'normal' was impossible...who wanted to anyway?

Business dealings and managing work was a struggle after that for it all seemed so slow and, more importantly, the withholding of information for personal gain seemed so futile and pointless. The scheming designs of those I was engaging for business seemed so clear and the shallowness of that mindset was just too mediocre to bear. I just wasn't one bit interested in lying and living with those who adopted that approach. It was hurting in ways that I can't describe; the silence within was getting disturbed every time I engaged in some form of personal gain. The voice inside, that silent witnessing state, was suddenly active and responding with alarming regularity and the more I listened to an intuitive knowing of what was right, the better life started to become.

I was also, for the first time in my life, clear about who I wanted to spend time with, who I wanted to do business with and with whom I wanted no contact. From a short-term business standpoint, there were losses to be made as business was refused and invitations declined for new partnerships and possibilities. The beauty was that the game started to become clear without any effort (fear or the need to grab the moment and make it certain) as what was not relevant just faded into irrelevance. This was also a time when I was made offers to merge my company with other entities and join hands for a bigger play. I just allowed what was right to show itself up rather than figure it out mentally. It wasn't that I had surrendered the mental faculties to some cold storage but rather they were available when needed. The heart was doing all that was needed, and effortlessly at that. During this stage, a lovely set of partnerships and new clients also came to the forefront, one of them being the Sunshine Group in India (interesting name too, potent with so many good possibilities). This was a client, the leaders of the business, whom I could invite home for a meal or make myself available for times when they needed me. Business wasn't the agenda in the main but what mattered was a relationship based on truth. Our firm was assisting them set up a four-star hotel in Mumbai, negotiating terms with a leading hotel services operator, the famed Taj Group of Hotels, as well as enabling them to raise capital in the future. It all seemed just right and they remain close friends even now. The big challenge was soon to come, however, when the bi-annual meetings or sharing of progress reports with the investors in my company came up. The need to look smart, cook the books and speak platitudes was just not worth the relationship I shared with them. It was never the case anyway but in the past there was always an air of optimism that was conveyed as the sentiment in the main. This time, however, I was clear that they had to know the whole nine yards, including my accident, the experience that followed and the aftermath of that on my life. I was refusing to take on assignments and opportunities that I felt needed a compromise in ethics and the investors were supportive, silently wishing that all would be well in time.

The 'remembrance' of the silence within was just too strong...the flavour intense, the feeling real

Turning back and getting entertained by short-term attention grabbers or getting back on the treadmill and living out additional dreams was just impossible for I had tasted the nectar of nectars and that, too, without any effort. It was almost as if a gift was made available, a window into another world or another dimension had opened up and then, once I had looked over the wall, looked over the illusory prison that I was in, there was no staying back. What I had read in some of the best books spoken or written by the Masters of our times or earlier seemed to make sense in one instant. It was an indescribable feeling and yet one where the draw for more was very, very strong. In one instant, life just made sense and everything looked just perfect. I had to, I felt deeply, find out more of the same. Little did I know then that that attitude itself was the barrier to experiencing the NOW. Speaking with some of my closest friends drew mixed reactions, while the seniors from my family were pensive and not very supportive of what I shared and what I felt I needed to search.

The business was not in the best of shape and the compromises required to get it back on track were just too much to go through. My health too was just about at some unhappy 50% performance and the traffic of thoughts relentless and varied, all with the potential to derail a steady state. I had to go out and know myself if there was anything beyond what I had experienced. This time though, the venturing out was not to be in a 'testing the waters' fashion, but a deep dive, holding nothing back. There wasn't much of a choice to be made from that perspective anyway. What was important was the well-being of my family, especially my kids, and I kept aside all I had in their name, converting all assets to cash (liquidity is a big bonus when dealing with change), asking my wife to take even greater responsibility in managing the home and our kids. I am grateful that we had the freedom to make such a choice although the upside wasn't a given. What would I find at the end of my search? What would I return to and back as? Would the prevailing conditions be different and unforgiving then? I had no answers but just a gut feeling that I had to go, for I had a momentary taste of freedom like never before.

Every moment is pregnant with immense possibilities; possibilities that shape up as attention alights on a thought. That quality of attention itself decides what is then experienced. That attention is, many a time, generated at a subconscious level. When a reference is taken from the past, there is one experience (a known one in most cases) and when the reference is taken from the future (an expectation), then again the experience is in the known dimension. This whole cycle of experiencing and being fulfilled or being frustrated is largely driven by the past, the future too is just a mixed bag of desires that are just meant as a compensation for what was lacking in the past. My life, in large part, seemed like a blur, a 'dash', if you will, from the time I was born (or from the time I remember my own space boundaries) and what had followed since then was just a relentless march without any real intent other than survival or, at times, just old-fashioned dominance. The constant barrage of memories of the past coloured the taste of what was offered in the present, so much so that the present was completely missed and the past reinforced and relived. The pain of being abused in the past made its presence felt through a complete distrust of the present and so many simple and innocuous relationships just fell by the wayside. The aftertaste then was a familiar one, that of being left alone to fend for myself. That was one part. Almost all accomplishments were with the single motive of ensuring a certain 'quality of life', a quality that was missing in the past. So in effect, all that was being experienced was just the past, all throughout. What if the attention was just on what was, as it (the moment) unfolded without any dilution from the past or the future? Could that be a possibility worth holding? Could that possibility involve any effort at all? Could the mind hold itself from its 'itch', its customary habit of coming in the middle? That was the biggest riddle of all, of finding that which did not need to be still to be still; that which was beyond words.

The question itself was the problem. What question was the right one? What quest would that lead me on? So, as is the case with the 'normal' world, I set about asking those in the know, spending time with those who felt they knew. I also started to spend time at courses that were seemingly designed to stimulate the process of a personal enquiry. The question that was not expressed but remained deep down within as an enigma was about my life itself. Why was I at war with myself? Taking that further raised many more questions. Why, in spite of having the world, it still wasn't enough (the James Bond movie came later) and it did not feel right? Why did I have the life that I had so far and what lay ahead? What was the source of true happiness? This 'rags to riches' or the 'humble beginnings in Mumbai to the priciest location in London' story was all fine for the outside world but what after all that? Had I stuck with the grind, I suppose I would have ended up sabotaging my life big-time; that was clear. There were so many examples of guys who began their life in the simplest of circumstances to then rise as gladiators and conquer the world only to then expose a chink in their armour and then fall from their high pedestals. This list of those who had fallen by the wayside was one that comprised not only those in the recent past but since time immemorial. The fall was almost always triggered by either an experimentation with drugs (to feel a new 'high'), or sex (to just 'escape' the world, driven by biological necessities and then perhaps mental afflictions) or money (a craze for the ephemeral, a taste for all things rich). I had to find that elusive elixir of peace. I just had to. Some of what is now to follow in this book isn't linear by way of timeline. Some of what transpired, what I engaged in, took place before the accident but for purposes of easy reading, it's included in one place, sequentially – but, as we all know, life is never sequential. Words can never really express a three-dimensional flow, one that includes the past, the future and the present too; story-telling is such an art. So there I was, putting away my life's content as well as what I had in my shirt and trouser pockets and being totally open for what it took to get freedom from the baggage (I labelled that baggage as 'societal conditioning').

Then started the looking up of meditation courses, ashrams, teachers and Masters, other seekers with whom to compare notes. What is more, I had my heart, or so I thought, to guide me.

That is the closest that I can describe how it felt.

BOOK TWO:
The Search, The Breakdown

The Lake Within

Silent, subtle and serene
Birds come, birds go, every time a new scene
Ripples begin, ripples end, every moment
a new form in place
The lake...just a pure witness, including, unattached,
an eternal space

Muddied waters in turbulent times
Bubbling waters in other climes
Rise and fall, a coming and going
The lake...just being, no doing

See it within, see it now
Let go of the push, let go of the rush
Come home finally, come home to yourself.

BOOK TWO: The Search, The Breakdown

Education in schools, as we know, is imparted in a linear manner. There are a few merits of that approach but also many a demerit. The biggest demerit is that that approach begins to dumb down the inherent intelligence within students as they start to just look for external approval as a mark of their progress. True learning is one where the inner intelligence wakes up to its own brilliance and participates with what is presented. I was clear from all the formal education that I had been through that I would not enrol in some 'spiritual' college or university or, for that matter, a course on psychotherapy. The latter to me felt dead, devoid of soul and not one that I had seen help those who were in need of fresh perspectives.

This 'search' itself is a conundrum. What is one searching for? Who is the one doing the 'searching'? Where does one start? How does one know with certainty that one has found what one is looking for? What happens after it (whatever that 'it' is) is found or known? Can one come back and be normal in the world? Is this (the quest for seeking) just a ruse to avoid taking responsibilities that are to be dealt with? What if I fail in this quest? What next? These and a million more questions arise, all from a state of fear and perhaps ignorance too and the only compass that can be truly trusted is the silent voice within. This is really a personal choice and I had made mine. To begin with, the external search was focused on becoming efficient in life to deal with the seemingly day-to-day demands of a competitive world but that gave way to an even more earnest one, that of wanting to transcend suffering and pain, all the success notwithstanding. The accident provided the impetus and a window into a different dimension.

This section and the chapters within will go back and forth on the various paths, nooks and crannies, watering holes and real resting places that I took over the years, not just after the accident but even before, a good two decades ago. It's important to cover all those for they all set the context for what was to follow. It will go over some of the absolutely interesting situations and people I encountered along the way; teachers, thugs, Masters and just some really helpful souls that all made the journey so worth it. They all remain in my heart and I have the utmost of gratitude to have met each one of them.

BOOK TWO:
The Search, The Breakdown

Chapter 1:
The search: questions, books, people, processes

Back to the 1990s and later...flashback time, India and the business school in Bangalore

I was in my mid-20s, studying at the Indian Institute of Management in Bangalore. It was a well-run institute that prided itself on being one of the very best in its business and the locale and the setting was just perfect. The course was spread over two years and had some 180-200 students from all parts of India, engaged in polishing their résumés to get better breaks in life. It was competitive but in a gentle sort of way. We had a break between the first and second years and I was in Mumbai, doing some form of project training with an engineering products company when I ran into an old batchmate of mine from my engineering days. The guy, as I remembered him from the 1983-1987 period was a docile, harmless and genial kind of a human being, not one to take up challenges and come into his own. I liked him for his simplicity and we had quite a few common interests in our teenage years, karate being one. The guy I met in 1991 in Mumbai was a different person from my old friend. In his place was someone who was self-assured, measured and yet fully engaged with his heart. The mental 'baggage' or the conditioning as it's termed, was always a burden that hindered free flow and full self-expression and in him, I saw glimpses of someone who had managed a breakthrough of sorts. I wanted to know more and that led me to my first pit stop, to refuel, re-calibrate and move ahead, at an event by one Landmark Education Corporation, called 'The Forum'.

'The Forum' and 'The Curriculum for Life'...a machine in its own class

This may raise many an eyebrow, as the event and Landmark as a firm does polarise how some people look at it. I don't wish to go into the plusses and minuses of either this or any of the pit stops for I will share what worked, what I picked up, what was good, and the rest I will just leave behind. The Forum, its curriculum (that word is a red herring, for how can there be a curriculum for life; perhaps this was a convenient word that stuck?) was almost like an encounter (and I am using that word mildly, for the real thing was even more stark and direct than that) and the process fairly well thought-through. The nature of the enquiry was such that, for the first time, it allowed for a 'compartmentalisation' of the baggage; smart terminology I must say and the process, the tools and techniques allowed for a recognition of many a repeating mind-pattern (baggage that caused short to long term pain). They had an efficient support structure (group work) that allowed for some ongoing mental gymnastics but as the group stages progressed the engagement started becoming anal at some point in time. As can be imagined, the groups became social-chat occasions (this was in the pre-Facebook days) and with that came personalities, moods and newer baggage. I was never the 'organisational' type and it was time to move on. I wasn't the least bit interested in being a part of any 'common-cause' group network. My school, engineering, business school friends, former colleagues and my family were enough for a lifetime, or so I thought. Nevertheless, that engagement, the Forum and its entire curriculum provided the means for a conversational ability as well as the capacity to engage in some serious introspection on topics that had no apparent answers.

A mental shift happened; from being tongue-tied to speaking about life with a fair degree of comfort. My relationship with my father started to feel better as there was a way to now catch many a 'mental programme' before it became a 'hurting pain' and a 'habitual act'; in effect, a degree of freedom I must say, did come about. A few new relationships took form, not based on any baggage but ones based on just plain aliveness. One such person, who remains a dear friend to this day, was a retired Indian Air Force pilot who had lost his eye in battle and now owns and manages a farm on the outskirts of Mumbai. He was also associated with Landmark as a leader, conducting events and guiding those participating to a deeper enquiry into the source of their own effectiveness. He was a large-hearted man and my conversations with him at the events, at his farm and over the phone made it clear that, while the Forum was great in its construct, I needed a much deeper look into the workings of the mind. Being competitive, coming out tops and making more money was never an issue but what was a mystery was why my life was the way it was and what was my purpose on this planet. The conversations with him led to many books and meditations. He was a mystic in his own way but at heart a true Parsi and a dear friend. Those in the international community that come closest to the Parsis by way of their attitude to life are the Greeks; same lifestyle and perhaps an equally interesting diet and set of social norms. He had a wide repertoire of books that he read and I used the time with him to explore what topics and writing styles appealed to me. The best part was that some of the books and the authors themselves spoke of other books that had been a source of inspiration or a repository of more information and that remark itself became a lead to more reading.

I bade goodbye to Landmark Education and moved on. I do share at length my experiences about The Forum but as I look at it, useful as it was and perhaps timely too, it was just smarter mind-stuff to deal with more mind-stuff; good in its place but perhaps limited in its expanse and flowering.

Two books stood out clearly. The first was a book titled *My Way: The Way of the White Clouds* by Osho, the much admired and yet controversial Pune-based Guru and the other was titled *Reiki* by Paula Horan, the lady who was held as a leading light in her field. The book by Osho was unlike anything I had read so far – the flow of words on the page, the seemingly wide array of topics that he covered with an ease unheard of and his method – unusual. It was all too much to just sample and leave behind. I had to know more but the social overtones against going 'public' about 'following' or at a very mild level visiting the Pune commune, were too high. I was up for it but felt I needed to know more, read more and form a view. They say in spiritual circles that there is a right time for everything and so it was. I just did not feel ready for a real and radical exploration. I remember my in-laws threw a fit when they saw the volume of Osho books in my home in Mumbai and I understood their sense of relatedness to what was happening and what could. Here I was, married to their daughter, and Osho was 'branded' by the media, as a 'sex-Guru'. Looking back, as I see the entire landscape now, it's so clear that he was misunderstood, a man so ahead of his time. 'Sex' is such a taboo topic, suppressed in many ways than one and it's a given that what is resisted will persist.

Reiki with Paula Horan...no talk, just silence and a focused intent

There was an advert in the local press in Mumbai that the famed teacher, Paula Horan, was visiting India and was offering courses that promised proficiency in Reiki. I had had a Reiki treatment once for healing my legs from the constant pain I was suffering and I was intrigued by the simplicity and the purity of the experience. I was up for meeting Paula. I had read her book and wanted to see what she had to offer that would make life better and easier to live. The day-long course was priced at some USD50 and I reached the venue, a rather sad-looking, run-down bungalow, where the drawing room was used as a makeshift seminar centre. Around 30 people had turned up, a mixed bunch from all walks of life: housewives, doctors, independent Reiki practitioners and a few that defied categorisation, me included. I did not know why I was there but it seemed and felt right to be there.

There were mattresses on the floor all laid out such that not an inch of floor space was without one and the people attending were all sitting in a circle, holding hands. This was my first of a million 'let's hold hands, connect and begin' starts and that felt good too. It's a bit overdone in spiritual circles though, and really not needed as a means to becoming silent. Just a simple attention to the breath is enough. Anyway, the long and the short of the course was that we had to give and receive 'treatments' which basically was no big deal other than holding the palms face down on different parts of the body and then allowing for a deep state of relaxation and healing to occur, the premise being that the 'giver's' body was the conduit for some Universal Life Energy to flow through. This ULF term was the first of the many times I would hear it. There was nothing to do other than be fully present while the treatment was given. This was the basic course and I suppose the follow up courses may be more advanced but it all felt too slow for my liking. It was super receiving a treatment but giving one, at least of this kind, wasn't one that appealed to me. My sister Yogita later became a Reiki Master in her own right and I was blessed to have been treated by her; a huge back pain that was refusing any form of treatment and medicine finally dissolved after a two-hour session. Paula herself was a nice human being, aware beyond just the course and its process. I liked her space, the energy she enabled in the room with all those around. This was also the first time that I was a part of a gathering that wasn't corporate in its outlook, which meant a mass of people who were present without ties, white shirts, black shoes and the lot and were present in sheer humility to receive something they considered valuable to their own personal growth. The energy, as I mentioned, was calm and flowing and it felt good. If this was what such events offered as a side-product or experience, I wanted more of it.

Yoga, pranayam and the first experience of being exploited...a sign of my own ignorance

As a working professional, whether at KPMG or Goldman Sachs or, indeed, running my own business, it was imperative to be at peak mental and physical fitness. I had joined a gym (the Holiday Inn in Mumbai, bless the staff, the trainers and the guy who kept the lemon juice container always full) where I was introduced to yoga and pranayama. A yoga instructor was conducting classes every alternate day. A good hour of yoga and a ten-minute pranayama was just the thing to start the day with. His commentary during the winding-down process, a guided meditation at the end, was the real thing. He seemed like a well-meaning fellow, well versed in the scriptures (reciting verses from the Bhagvad Gita, the holy book revered in India) and was quite good at contextualising his commentary to the situation. He had another role to play in the evening (nothing murky or sinister) where he held short discourses in rich homes, Gujarati or Jain families (one of the many communities in India), where he'd hold a small prayer, a discourse followed by a distribution of fruits. It all seemed harmless and perhaps even educative (not a bad combination I felt then) till he offered a one-on-one guidance for many an unanswered spiritual question. That was heavy stuff in those days and so I committed to a special pooja (prayer), which meant dressing up in whites, fasting for the day and chanting some mantras at his home at a chosen time in the evening for what seemed like an eternity. My belief then was that all this effort would perhaps, with his guidance, result in some sort of a 'seeing', a 'mini awakening'. The gifts that I had brought along, including a white kurta (an Indian dress worn at festive occasions) that was to be worn by me after my 'graduation' or so I thought, were quietly passed on to his waiting family members and that was the last time I met him. His yoga skills were great, of a very high order and remain with me until now, but that was all there was to him. He was a mere technician; nothing beyond that.

Vipasana meditation...a silent sitting for twelve days but too early, too soon

A very dear friend of mine had just completed a Vipasana course (a ten-day silent meditative technique supposedly offered by the Buddha) and he spoke at length about his experience. Our relationship was such that I decided to give it a try (he and I were classmates from kindergarten). York in the UK is a lovely little city and the venue chosen was housed in a church, a beautiful setting which had rooms for the attendees. This course is offered on a no-fee basis and participants then have the freedom to donate whatever they can afford, or feel is appropriate, after the course is over. This, I felt then and still do, is truly a very noble way of connecting to the highest good in all those connected to the event; bless the organisation and their founder and all those involved in the delivery of what is perhaps a very, very simple, but a highly impactful process. The rooms were luxurious – soft beds and bathtubs, although the course was supposed to be minimalist in its origins and delivery. Men and women are housed in different set-ups and the meditation hall too is demarcated such that, for the entire duration of the course, one does not have the chance of encountering anyone from the opposite sex. It was a bit different at this course as the venue was a hired one, but they do ensure strict adherence to norms at their centres across the world, or so I am told. Anyway, my roommate was part-busker and part-hippy, or both depending on the weather. The silent ten day period was torture to begin with, the first three days in the main, and then there was a settling into a 'no rush' state after that. Seeing the roommate sample my shaving kit, use the entire length of the wardrobe and more was a bigger obstacle; so much so for connecting with the Divine within in deep silence.

All things considered, this was a good course; a bit tiring and torturous, the silence immediately afterwards was noticeable but I felt a bit vegetative. The founder has done a great deal of good by preserving the basic tenets of the course and making it accessible to the world but, in my experience, it isn't for everyone. It surely is one of the highest and purest of meditative techniques but unless an emotional catharsis has taken place, unless the flood of desires has been exhausted, it just isn't possible to be true to the path. When the fire of desires is running rampant within, any amount of 'pure witnessing' just doesn't make the grade at that juncture. Buddha, before he embarked on his quest, was Siddhartha the Prince and had access to the best of the best and it was only after he was 'done' with the subtlest and most sublime of luxuries that his attention settled on that that was transient but certain. I won't go into his life here for it's a well-known story but the main reason to giving this twist was to make the point that it's important to know what is right and when. Silent sitting could take a lifetime to quench the fires within and there are faster, better and more proven ways available; silent sitting after that can be a different experience. It's like wearing a white linen shirt and white cotton trousers on a lovely warm summer evening in sunny Corfu in Greece but having a bath and getting a good wash before can make it a super experience. Emotional catharsis first before the silent sitting helps.

Fast forward to London...Goldman Sachs and in between two worlds

Life at Goldman Sachs was a rush of sorts; checking voicemails every four hours during the day (first thing in the morning and last thing at night – a great system but a bit taxing, overdone and perhaps over-abused) and the seemingly endless and at times pointless preparation of 'material for discussion' with CEOs. If that wasn't enough pressure, there was the '360 degree' feedback compiled from at least 25 reviews that dictated the need and the direction of improvement that everyone had to be open to. The in-house training was almost devoid of anything 'right-brained' as the focus was on precision and efficiency in implementation.

Not many in the corporate world ever overtly share their personal growth needs or the stuff they explore to meet those needs, for it all sounds 'touchy-feely', much against the usual macho look that is projected. Most burn-outs begin here and if only corporate environments were supportive in listening to what was beyond the obvious when it came to an individual's performance or lack of it, we'd see a more consistent performance from the individual. Organisations that have a more feminine outlook are creative and open, generally show a greater executive longevity and an overall sense of well-being within.

The role that I was entrusted with was a bit boring to say the least, but what was remarkable was the expansiveness of the conversations that one of the guys I worked with, the team leader, managed to enable. He was a real player in the sense that many of the situations, any really, failed to shake his inner silence and that was an experience to see first-hand. My reading of all books alternative and those that were to do with personal breakthroughs continued at a regular pace, much more than the attention I was giving at work. It was all good but there are limits to how much, if any, can be assimilated by just reading. Intellectual engagement is one important aspect in creating the conditions for a breakthrough but the real thing is the actual commitment to the possibility. Reading such books on long flights to Seoul or Sydney was one thing but it all kind of faded into the background when the battle began the next day at work. The relentless nature of the work at Goldman Sachs meant that all things spiritual were kept aside for review at a later point in my life and sheer effectiveness became the mantra to target.

NLP with Richard Bandler and Anthony Robbins...effective but not what I was looking for

This technique, NLP or neuro-linguistic programming, was a much talked about one in the late 1990s and early 2000s. It was presented to the world as a seemingly innovative approach to 'emotionally relating' to the world, but the focus in the main was on subtle persuasion and that term created an inner dissonance in me. It kind of felt like manipulation but some of the guys I had worked with swore by its efficacy.

There was a seven-day intensive (this word 'intensive' is so misused) course with Richard Bandler in India, a portly fellow with a pony tail, who spoke so fast that hardly anyone would have understood what he was saying. That perhaps was a part of the process but the event was a circus of sorts, attended by those from all walks of life: a few CEOs, many hundreds of trainers and a 'holy man' who now has a large fan following or, should I say, devotees. The work seemed OK and did pay dividends at work and elsewhere. The desire to go further and explore the depths of this art (the founders call it a science but deliver in an art form) took me to London to a three-day specialised course by Bandler. This was attended by a smaller crowd of 30 or so that had a distinct British touch and the event enabled many a possibility at work and in other aspects of my life.

The course by Anthony Robbins in London at the huge ExCel Centre that housed nearly 8,000 attendees at that event was one to experience, again for similar reasons, for it provided a number of tools (language and techniques) to dissect the past and then arrange the pieces for a vibrant tomorrow. The event was conducted in a very slick manner, almost Hollywood-style, with the right conversations and body movements that allowed for the required emotions to show up, supported with appropriate music at the right decibel levels and giant screens to provide a 'larger than life' experience. The course did have an impact on my life financially (I was promoted to Executive Director and also earned a huge bonus that year) and otherwise. The guy has a way to share his energetic presence that is in its own class.

As I step back and look at what NLP was for me, I can say that the work has merit (the social overtones against its origins and its founders notwithstanding) but it is at a mental level and my search was in finding something that was lasting and did not add to the separation that was already so evident in my life. As a process, NLP was OK but it wasn't the door opener, the key to the inner kingdom that the real Masters down the ages spoke about. To be fair, neither of the trainers nor any of the better books promised anything spiritual; far from it, the work they offered was to make one effective in life and for that, I suppose, they do hold their own places in the sun.

Osho...a change of name, maroon robes and an experience of 'no mind'

Books have a static way of delivering an experience and at some level they just can't deliver the truth. A book takes a few sentences, a whole chapter or for that matter a good 300 pages to convey something that is inherently very simple. Try explaining love; try putting it into words and you will see the hopelessness of the effort, while at an experiential level no words are needed, just a knowing happens and then there is a perceptual shift. So is the case with many of the books in the Mind-Body-Spirit section. Reading books written by Osho is one thing; being in his commune and listening to his discourses and seeing him on screen is another. Although I had read many of his books and listened to his recordings, the experience of hearing him speak about the mundane, the commonplace and the esoteric, laced with humour and the silence that followed during and after his discourse, was something different. This I liked; actually, it was more than liking, it just felt right somewhere, at a place beyond words and beyond logic, those two included anyway, but much beyond. J Krishnamurthy's books were also engaging and thought-provoking, but to me they seemed cerebral, at least at that point in time in my life. Osho's approach to me felt 'whole body' and nothing was excluded.

The first taste of a totally different approach to breaking the pattern or knowing a 'no mind' state was through meditation technique by name Dynamic Meditation. This was the complete opposite of all that was believed about the process of meditation. This was catharsis of a kind I had never experienced before; a marathon run, a 50km bike ride or an hour-long session with an 'ex-athletic champ turned trainer' could come close but only just. The difference was that this, the Dynamic Meditation, was one where I was fully conscious. I just liked the simplicity of the process and also the fact that it has a 'rebel' streak to it.
Osho's name did, and still does, raise many an eyebrow and there are high social overtones against his work largely because of his views on sex. Many in the media and the world

at large had labelled him a 'sex guru' but I wasn't bothered about anyone's opinion. Those close to me were a bit aghast that I was dipping into dangerous waters but, true to form, none suggested an alternative path from a state of knowing. The usual 'stick with it' or 'this is life' or 'take another holiday' came up as the simpler options but there was no conviction behind those words. In effect, what the world was suggesting was that I take another pill to relieve me of the symptoms (the restlessness) but none went so far as going to the roots. 'Sex' as a word has a radical effect on people and in my view, people focus on what is inside of them; Osho was just an excuse for them, those who took offence to his opinions. My intention to break the old limiting mental patterns and the intensity behind that was such that I just did not bother about what the world had to say and, quite frankly, the world had no answers anyway. I was loath to stick to the straight and narrow for reasons I have mentioned earlier and this, Osho's work, seemed radical and logical at the same time, focused and expansive at the same time too. So Dynamic Meditation it was for a straight seven days from 6:00 a.m., and the day seemed surprisingly light after that. Food tasted better, there was slowness in everything, a deliberate comfortable one that was distinct, and music sounded even more melodious, not just that which my portable belted out, but which was always on as I made my walks to the commune, to my hotel room and all in between. There was a schedule or a calendar of events planned for every day that was available for those in the commune to participate in. I chose to sample all that was available and then decided what felt good for a second helping. My favourite in those days was something called a Dance Celebration, a seemingly innocuous but subtle art form, where some really divine music was played in the open and those interested just danced to the tunes, danced without a partner and danced without a care for how they looked and appeared. This was just a perfect meditation for it felt like being back in my childhood, in school in the days when I used to get out in the rain and sing alone, get wet and soak with the elements. There was another favourite of mine called the Laughter Meditation where hundreds of seekers and meditators laughed their guts out for no reason followed by a silent state of witnessing. That got me cracking up first and then relaxing to a level that was intoxicatingly delicious. The evenings were reserved for a communion, a nice word this, with Osho himself on a wide screen, and that was a perfect end to the day. There was the odd evening party, a harmless way to engage in some lighthearted fun or listen to some creative performance that made for a complete meal. I was beginning to like the sheer rejoicing of my ordinariness for the first time and no one really bothered about who the other person was, most just celebrating their own uniqueness. In the midst of all this, I met many an interesting seeker; a high court judge from Brazil, a scientist from Germany, an Israeli couple who were in the hospitality business, a writer from the UK, a retired banker from the USA, a guy from Infosys (one of the leading Indian IT companies) and others. During our chats, it dawned on me that they were all lovely souls, wanting or waiting for a breakthrough in their lives and this was their 'dip' in waters outside of the known.

The beauty of the meditations at the commune and at the other centres where I spent time partaking of what was on offer was its simplicity. Bringing a 'witnessing' quality to daily life and being total while living it out were the two aspects that started to grow on me as a result of the time I spent at the commune, engaging in many of the meditations that Osho had suggested. The three foundation ones appealed to me deeply and each meditation course did its bit to alter my perceptual frame as I started to experience deeper states of relaxation and a general letting go of the need to prove or protect myself at the shortest possible opportunity. That itself was a life and half saved or so it felt. The techniques were inherently very simple, involved no conversations of any kind but just a period of deep catharsis followed by a silent witnessing stage. Simple as it may sound, I was amazed at its impact on making daily life such a blissful living experience.

I was experiencing long bouts of 'no mind', entering a gap between the relentless thoughts that seemingly make their way to centre stage for attention. The body too was responding just fine. There was no escapism at all for I was 100% present to what was on offer as a process; the basic meditative techniques that involved a conscious expression of either laughter, anger, sorrow, pain, gibberish or silence. What was unique about the entire set of techniques was its simplicity. One could just go through the process without the need for any complex instructions or a long-winded explanation and I liked that. This 'throwing you back to yourself' or 'turning in' were terms often used in self-help books and they surely seemed to have some magic in them. The meditative states did allow a window into a world that was not known to me until then. The experience during some of the processes was one of remembrance of nothing specific but a kind of an expansive view in which all was held but nothing particular was in focus. The food at the commune too was very nourishing; simple and vegetarian, served at the counters, waiting to be sampled. The day was filled with meditative techniques each an hour long, interspersed with breaks for meals, and with the kind of flexibility available it reminded me of my childhood at my grandmother's home; a whole day of play and small breaks for meals. There was a tarot card deck kept on a table that one could sample for free, a café that dished out snacks in an open-air setting with loads of trees to sit under and sanyasins (that dreaded word to the outside world), a harmless and entertaining bunch who dotted the place with maroon robes. The sea of maroon during the day or white in the evening was another experience of merging into a bigger flow as no one really bothered about explaining who he or she was and no one really cared either. As the trips to the commune increased, I got to know some of them and realised they (the sanyasins) came from all walks of life: professionals of the highest level to those managing a living as teachers, shopkeepers and the like. It almost felt that the whole world had descended on one place for seeking something beyond the mundane. This may not necessarily be the case with all but it seemed so for most of those I met.

One aspect that rankled outsiders, and still does, was that sanyasins changed their name to a different one, signifying a dropping of the most basic of identifications. This wasn't and isn't a 'must do' for those in the commune but for me the process seemed logical and I was ready to go the mile. So then started the search for a name, one that I felt epitomised my search and so Ekant it was, pronounced 'ay-kaanth' and it meant 'solitude'. The supportive name I chose was Dhyan which meant 'meditation' and the combined name meant 'the one who meditates in solitude'. So far so good and it all seemed manageable; the sanyasin community seemed like one happy family. In the commune and outside of it, a garb was available as Ekant had no history, no baggage and it felt perfect; the mental state of being without baggage, without pretensions, masks and more. The sanyas ceremony too was a unique experience in that the one thing I remember was getting loads of hugs from other sanyasins who had no personal agenda (at least that is what I am inclined to believe) but to just rejoice in the moment. The only other time I remember so many people celebrating my birthday (!), was when I was four or five years of age, all assembled and drinking loads of carbonated drinks and chatting about 'stuff' and whose faces seemed like masks in a Tibetan shop; the masks are better, as they are silent, they sit silently on a wall and are a good five to seven feet away rather than on the ground. This transition to Ekant was one that worked, as the conversations that followed were about seeking and replete with simple life experiences shared by those on the path. I was lucky to meet some really meditative souls for whom laughter and aliveness was just a way of life. The process of engaging in many of the meditations at the commune as well as meeting many seekers who had their own stories and insights to share provided a potent mix for a complete overhaul of how I lived my life. There were scores of new techniques that I was trying and it all seemed like there was good progress being made. The conversations with other seekers were getting relevant, engaging and many a new social group was being formed, almost by default.

However, life outside, the business side of things, was still the same or getting a bit out of sync. There came a time when I was juggling a business, doing transactions, reading self-help books on flights as well as shareholder agreements and term sheets, listening to meditative tapes and also voicemails, being a father and a householder and a sanyasin at the same time; it all seemed like one heavy act to sustain. The trouble was, the business part was the act while the sanyas part was borne out of a personal longing. The former was driven by societal demands, conditioning, dreams and more while the latter was based on a knowing that life was short and there was more to it than just eking out a living.

This was the dilemma; torn within and without.

BOOK TWO:
The Search, The Breakdown

Chapter 2:
Encounters of a tantric kind: satoris, openings, possibilities

Tantra, the dangerous path...from indirect to direct

The search with Osho went deeper and deeper and it felt just right all along, as my health was getting back to normal and just the right set of people were making their presence felt in my life for no effort on my part, ranging from clients to close friends. I was in deep gratitude for what was happening but the mind was still not satisfied that it had found a way, a path to bliss.

The mind always searches for a 'way out' and so it was here, albeit unconsciously. Grander designs of a 'purpose' or a 'perfect role for me and my life' were all thoughts that make their way up through the bubbling waters; rather, these very thoughts cause the still waters to bubble up and the turmoil continues. However, the universe or existence has no purpose; it just IS. Purpose is a product of the mind, a mental creation with its genesis in the thought 'I am separate from...' and 'I choose to...'. Therein lies the misery. It works for a while but the cycle continues. The seemingly mindful state of engaging in one dream after the other and experiencing a state of incompletion was clear to me.

My tryst with the meditative or spiritual side of life was so far inconclusive in the sense that it all seemed OK while I was 'in the process' but the harsh realities of the world outside seemed ready to make their presence felt as soon as I donned my suit and tie. In the midst of many a conversation with fellow seekers and teachers, I happened to meet one soul by the name of Jeeva Ananta, a lovely lady who was perhaps in her 60s but looked like she was just turning 40. She was about to commence a course on Tantra, that so misunderstood, misused and abused word in the West and now the East too, that was titled 'Tantra - A Journey Within'. In my conversations with her, there was something in her eyes and her presence that made me trust her word. She spoke with effortless ease about the commune, her life experiences and what she felt would be a good process for me to go through – Tantra. I had read Osho's books on Tantra, especially the one that was considered the best in its class, titled *The Book of Secrets* and it was on my mind to explore what this art form was. The commune was loath to allow an Indian into any of its Tantra courses as the social overtones against the art form were very high and the social upbringing that most had within India did not support a 'witnessing' of what was a highly meditative and a very direct process. I won't go into an evaluation of why the commune adopted such a posture but I do see the relevance of the mechanism they have set forth, one that perhaps ensures that the process delivers its best to the intended participants. So Tantra it was and I was ready that morning, clean-shaven, washed and in a fresh maroon robe.

This, as many may know, is an art form that uses a meditative set of techniques and is one of the most direct of paths; walking the edge, for there is no place to hide or contemplate as it works directly (focuses attention) on the senses. Those who know, know and those who don't just conjecture as to what it may be. To me, as I see it now, it was and is one of the most direct and riskiest of paths to a state of 'no mind'. I will elaborate later on why I see it as risky. Tantra is perhaps the most esoteric of all spiritual practices as it takes a totally contrary route to awareness, directly into the realms of unreasonable happiness. The premise of the path is that our sense organs are outwardly focused and always engaged in keeping us 'stuck' with the world of desires and aversions, towards desires and away from aversions; either a 'liking' or a 'deep dislike' of what we see, hear, taste, smell or feel by way of touch. In that state, there is no real freedom for the outcome is pre-determined (a projection) and the senses are just reporting what is already a decided state. Almost all other meditative techniques are such that they allow for and are aimed at a settling of the mind (witnessing) and so are a step away but Tantra works directly on the senses (embracing all that is) by witnessing (hopefully, if taught well and if the seeker too is of the right make-up), by bringing full consciousness to the act of sensing itself, to the moment of sensing such that the desire, the experiencing of the desire and the witnesser of what is unfolding are known as One; the knowing of the macrocosm through the knowing of the microcosm. As you can now see, it is devoid of lengthy discourses and inane conversations and is about engaging directly and with full awareness in what is an otherwise unconscious or 'programmed' process. The nature of the mind is such that we are either in the past or in the future. Seeking in the beginning, in most cases, is based on the admission of time, thus causing a separation between us (the seeker) and that which we seek (us again). Tantra is the most direct way to cutting that gap, for it uses the body as an instrument in being in the now. No theory will make that an experience, for it just can't be explained.

Social overtones against the art form earlier took it 'underground' in India. The lack of clear ways to measure its effectiveness allowed a raft of 'Tantra quacks' down the ages, and even now, to conduct 'classes' and because of them, this art form continues to be seen as one with a 'dark side'. Most such quacks aren't grounded in the art of silent meditation, aren't initiated into it by a real Master and have no personal ethics about the risks they place on those attending. There is also much to say about how the art is offered and without a set of guidelines the standards vary; from the sublime to the plain mediocre or, even worse, the downright ridiculous. This is more so in the USA where this art form has taken a sexual overtone. Most of the teachers (!) spend a few weeks in India, align themselves to some school or other and then offer that as a course or a practice. The immediate effects of playing (!) with sexual energy are obvious and a general sense of euphoria is always a result. Most miss the point (those attending the courses) and then descend into a vacuous state where their intellect gets further eroded as they become pleasure seekers and course junkies; a path that is devoid of consciousness. The mind has its ways to convince that all is well. Students do get the teachers they deserve, so I suppose there should be no complaints if the process isn't working out. Tantra is a dangerous path if practised without the right teacher (without the appropriate disciplines and practices in place) as is true of any science. It's also the most direct path when learned under an accomplished teacher. I have been on this path, starting with a harmless but well thought-through introduction by a teacher in India then to schools in the UK to finally Varanasi, where the latter brought a deep surrendering, devotional and witnessing element to an otherwise fiery process and I can only speak from my personal experience that it isn't one bit as the media portrays it. In the era of instant noodles, double cheese-burgers and ready-to-eat meals, most art forms are bound to suffer, for the attention is on the grosser elements.

The deep dive into Tantra...bringing consciousness to all body needs

The period of consciously experimenting with this art form was intense, spread over a good two-year period. What struck me as unique was the sheer simplicity of the processes, for there were many meditative techniques to go through. Devoid of more mind-stuff to deal with mind-stuff, this was about just embracing the NOW and witnessing all that arose including the mind's tendency to get attracted to or repulsed from what it was in touch with. I clearly remember the first time I experienced a sparking of the senses, something akin to a 'power surge'; a distinct feeling of aliveness and watchfulness, a midnight vigil of sorts. I won't go into the actual processes that ensued in each of the events for, as I mentioned, reading about it (Tantra) is one thing, experiencing and knowing it is another.

The courses were led in a way that allowed for clear boundaries to be defined between participants so that each one could feel safe and secure as the processes unfolded. There was also a clear and explicit statement mentioned in each of the courses that there would be no intimacy of any kind that involved genital contact. That perhaps set to rest expectations and must have allowed a certain kind of community to form under the tutelage of the school that offered the course. The Vigyan Bhairav Tantra, that immensely beautiful and powerful book, the supposed repository of all things tantric, has a number of sutras or meditative techniques of which only a few concern some level of intimacy. Only those few get attention, or at least what they profess to cover and the rest are overlooked. There are tomes written about this art form, most of which are quite pedestrian, plagiarised and re-plagiarised and it's best to avoid 'microwave' products. The media too has a way of showcasing anything related to Tantra which unfortunately has become synonymous with all things 'sex'.

The change was discernible...and effortless at that

Many things changed in the aftermath of the Tantra courses that I was attending. Music for one clearly became a living experience, so did conscious eating become a meditative opportunity as did a general slowing down of everything in life. From a fast-paced and adrenalin heavy state, the drop into a slow (not lazy but relaxed) and blissful state was noticeable.

I vividly remember the time when music came to life in my life, in a small hamlet in the Himalayas, in Bhagsu. The 'before' and 'after' states were clearly stark. I had a collection of perhaps 140 songs on my iPod; after that, and perhaps a good six months from then my collection had swelled to 12,000 with music from all over the world. A Vigyan Bhairav Retreat had just been over. This was in Dharmshala and I was loath to travel back to Delhi to get stuffed by the 'sight, sound and smell' show that is so true of most cities in India, save a few. India is an awesome country with an outstanding legacy: festivals, colours, people, cuisine, beauty, the wisdom of the ages, an alive feminine energy. I could go on and fill an entire book about what I love about India but the state of infrastructure within the country is pathetic, shameful and doing grave injustice to its potential. So I took to the hills, the Himalayas rather, travelling further north, to McCleodganj and then to Bhagsu, a small hamlet, halfway down the peaks and halfway up; just perfect. The physical, mental, emotional and spiritual state was one of high sensitivity to the environment, grounded and chilled, and in that state I ambled across the village main street to see a poster that advertised an informal music event scheduled for that evening. With no other agenda planned for the evening, it seemed like a good thing to try out and so I went and was blown away by one of the singers who became a friend and who then shared her music collection with me (bless iPod, Apple, iTunes, for you were the passage, the bridge between the old and the new). She sings at the Inspiral Lounge in Camden Town in London and has a voice that brings an awareness of that which can't be verbalised, almost using sound to give an experience of silence. That same evening I learned of an informal music 'jam-nite' on the top of a mountain plateau and was invited by some of the music lovers; bless their tribe, for they make the world a better place. Post-dinner, I walked up a few hundred steps, large boulders that made for a natural 'staircase' to reach a half-cleared mountaintop. A mid-sized space, perhaps equal to quarter of a football pitch, seemed to have been cleared of clumps of grass and rocks, although the vestiges of the effort seemed apparent. There was a campfire in place, in the centre, and a good 100-120 person crowd had gathered around the fire in three groups with a few floating souls who ambled from one group to another. There were music groups; one that was expressing sufi music over string instruments, the other Indian classical over flute and percussion and the last one a motley bunch with a number of musical instruments that I had never seen or heard before. Each group was playing their own tune and then handing over to the next and all this happened without words, without any gestures; just a dance of silence and sound, and over a period of 30-35 minutes it all came together, not in an organised way but just guided by some Divine Intelligence (let this word not be a distraction here for the focus is on the experience and not on what may have caused that), a melody that was alive like no other, a birthing if you will, unbelievably lilting and intoxicating. It had just about everything and I lost track of time (as I now recount the experience) and was just the music. All thoughts, aspirations, pain and everything for those few moments just seemed to vanish and in their place were just silence, wonder and an expansiveness that I can't describe but one that included everything: stars, moon, campfire, clumps of grass, rocks, mountains, the crowd, the musicians. A cloud had burst somewhere, a thunder had cracked, a lightning had struck somewhere and there was joy for no reason, just no reason.

This was similar to the state I remembered when I had the accident. There was just pure gratitude for being alive and for the gift of this experience; that of seeing the melody build as a delicate dance between sound and silence, between yang and yin, between male and female, between positive and negative, between control and freedom, take to form and the dance was happening on the outside and within me too. My collection from then on has gone to over 12,000 tracks, from tango to Afro, from hip hop to reggae, from jazz to Indian classical and more. It all came to bear when I met my music guru in Mumbai with whom I am learning vocal Indian classical and now sing at the events in which I participate.

Besides music, there were similar moments of touching states unknown, consciously so. The art of eating consciously, sampling each bite in the slowest and most deliberate manner, allowed for a state of silence; just me and the food and then just the tasting itself. I can tell you that being fed nutritious food, that too when blind-folded, can have a magical effect on the sense of taste and smell. The added effect of being blindfolded creates an eager anticipation of something that is beautiful but unknown and, in that state, one is just total with the experience. There is no separation between the one who is eating, what is being eaten and the experience of eating itself. All merge into one with just the experience remaining. The sense of touch, when engaged in a conscious manner, can allow for transcendence to a state that is 'no mind' too. What started to happen as a by-product of attending the courses was that the body was getting deeply relaxed in the NOW state and the mind was just beginning to notice the sheer bliss of just being without wanting or resisting. There was a deliberateness that I was noticing take shape in my life, an apparent easy pace in almost all aspects of my life and time seemed to be just slowing down.

This was a taster and not the real thing as it was a technique that allowed a window, a path to a state of 'no mind'. The risk of getting addicted to the process itself and forgetting the objective as to why the process was adopted in the first place was high. The challenge was to remain true to the path and not get addicted to what some of the 'taverns' on the path offered as an excuse. While all the plusses of the path were manifesting in form, there remained the feeling deep down that I still was far away from the Truth as the so-called effortless way wasn't a felt experience, wasn't a natural state. There was still fear of the unknown; a thousand fears making themselves heard above the din of the day over a lost moment or many a time in the dark of the night, when some unexplained dream sequence started to shape up in a weird way, highlighting some really bizarre twist and turn that wasn't palatable to the mind. I knew that all such 'visions' were really projections of the mind itself, the ego wanting to hold back to its earlier state as the 'decider', choosing what was good and what wasn't. My life though, the way I was living it, was actually a death of the ego in small and large doses. That was all very well but I was also clear that this anxiety-ridden state was also not tenable for long. If the path was right, if the intention was pure, then the results had to be positive, satvic, and a general sense of well-being was to surely follow. I was loath to believe any past-life regression expert or some spirit-talker or anyone for that matter who created more rubbish through even greater use of uncertainty, language and terms where I just had to be a silent spectator. I just wasn't in the mood to trust some soothsayer or some 'Baba' or 'holy man' who could speak from or about the future. There were many of those kinds that I met but, as luck would have it, our chemistry never matched and they ended up avoiding me. I have a host of hilarious anecdotes of such interactions with them that I share in the course of my conversations with people.

So there I was – a long journey through many a maze, loads of new experiences and techniques to share and use but that state of feeling a deep bliss that I had tasted during the accident and other meditative moments during the retreats that I had attended that was still elusive. It still wasn't a normal state. It was clear that what I was doing so far had outlived its purpose and I needed a break from that routine. Something new had to be tried out, something even more radical.

Hungry for more but tired of the old; that is how it felt and it wasn't some wanton experimentation that I would go for but something far more tested and widely accepted.

BOOK TWO:
The Search, The Breakdown

Chapter 3:
The real breakdown: darkness after dawn

A hiatus from trudging the pilgrim's path...to an experimentation in silence

Life until then was filled with reading books, having a few daily morning meditations and attending courses that looked relevant. The social network had expanded to well over 1,000, largely seekers from all parts of the world whom I had met at courses or later at events. The odd meeting up for a buffet lunch at Vita Organics in Soho or Yantra near Oxford Circus or for a cup of tea at the Inspiral Lounge in Camden Town did allow for a sharing of what worked, what was the latest and who were perhaps the better of the teachers in all things alternative. The London Mind-Body-Spirit Festival was another watering hole which drew seekers and practitioners, goods providers and traders in all things alternative in the UK and perhaps Europe too. But I was getting a bit restless with all this, for I did not want to just be floating in ether (although we actually are, in a manner of speaking and I am completely relaxed with that now) and be seeking all my life. I was wanting to see tangible results, although the definition of what tangible means on such a path itself is an impossibility. So, as is the case when faced with uncertainty, doubling the intensity of the efforts and becoming righteous about what was being pursued was a given outcome.

Sun gazing...to tap some unknown force apparently

As a part of my experimentations and meeting new people, I was invited to an event where   a speaker was to share his life story and this seemed interesting. He was a 'sun gazer' who was famed for gazing at the sun for such long durations every morning and evening that the effort had made a significant shift in his inner bio-chemistry. He was perhaps 70+ years of age but in physical terms looked much, much younger. He was also known to have gone off normal food and was subsisting on just sun gazing and water. It looked too simple and clever at the same time to be true but his effort apparently was being researched and closely followed by a leading scientific organisation; that made the difference and so I went. I listened to his talk and decided to give his process a real try. The steps were very simple: ten seconds of sun gazing the first day with an addition of ten seconds each day that followed until one reached about 44 minutes. His claim was that life would alter dramatically at that stage. The room had over 300-400 people from all walks of life and that itself was some sort of a community feeling, one that hindered any scientific questioning. He spoke with authority that there would be no side effects (!) as long as one managed to complete this process at sunrise and close to sunset. Now, London is not famed for the sunny days it gets, let alone allowing for a view of a lovely sunrise or a settling sunset. The weather gods were kind and with the level of travel I was managing to India and back and to other cities in Europe, it was somehow possible to make the time for this process and it cost nothing. With complete trust (blind at that), I stuck to the straight and narrow and had managed to get to a good 30 minutes of non-stop sun gazing per day at the suggested times. Although I wasn't experiencing any dramatic perceptual shifts in the level of my consciousness, I was feeling tired and the eyes looked a bit 'haggard'. I was still determined to get to the magical 44 minutes. One thing I must add though; sun gazing for a few moments in the early hours of dawn or the late hours of dusk and reciting a sun salutation mantra can be very therapeutic in ways that I can't describe but only know as my own experience. That was just the perfect input required; a moment of witnessing, a moment of silent gratitude and a moment of celebration along with the one life-giving source that we all know and see every day. It's perhaps one of the very best ways to start the day.

The Holy Scriptures, chanting mantras and more...following tradition in search of the Truth

The one constant refrain that religious leaders and healers made during discourses, meditation camps or just over simple conversations, was to mention and recite verses from the Holy

Scriptures such as the Bhagvad Gita, the Dyaneshwari, the Upanishads, the Bible and more. I had not yet paid any real attention to any of these holy books but had, in many a setting at home or in temples, sung along a mantra or recited a prayer. The experience at home as a child saying my prayers with my mother and my sisters was a very real fond one to have. The amount of stuff I had explored in search of the Truth was such that all of it remained relevant but did not settle my thirst. Conversations with those who were leading events wasn't helping as they would end up sharing more of the same and by now I had become well-versed with the lingo and the mindset of what it took to run events of the kind I was participating in. A few teachers were inviting me to participate as an assistant or a co-teacher and while all that was good, I did not really care much about what it offered as a possibility. My own silence wasn't of the kind that was untouched by any disturbance and I was not in the slightest of moods to fake anything. This wasn't some corporate treadmill where I was being watched and judged on some formal ranking system, where I could tweak the settings to manage the way ahead. Here I was the watcher and I did not want to delude myself into some other state I was not in. In such a half-baked state I must say, I then looked to the scriptures to share their light on the right path for me to follow.

Reading the scriptures, starting with the Bhagvad Gita, seemed a workable idea and so after my morning yoga and pranayam I started an hour of reading the holy book. Somewhere, halfway through the book, another suggestion came up from one of the teachers I was close to, to chant mantras along with all the meditation techniques that I was engaging in every day. My mother used to recite prayers every morning before leaving for work and every evening before serving food to us all and I was a co-singer with her on many of those occasions. It seemed well within the realm of possibility and I was also asked by a teacher to chant at specific times during her meditation events. There was also the opportunity of chanting at the London Mind-Body-Spirit Festival to inaugurate a session, but it felt like it was just an act to go through. I won't go into the intricacies of the various mantras, the effects of chanting (although chanting works, as it's a form of music) for there is so much nonsense written about chakras, the energy centres that correspond to the endocrinal system within the body, and about Kundalini energy, that it's best to experience the Truth through experience, through knowing first-hand. Anything I say will be just another concept and will get in the way. In the larger scheme of things, it's not really important to know any of this stuff at all and anyone who professes to be an 'expert' is really making use of your ignorance and gullibility. Just be conscious and that is enough. More on that later, though.

Candle gazing as a technique...one-pointedness of the mind

The search for techniques that I could do at home or when travelling, those that required minimal effort by way of resources and rituals, was a constant one. It was during a series of related conversations with a fellow seeker and a yoga master in India that I was introduced to 'candle gazing'. This meditation is also known by the name 'tratak' but I won't go into a detailed explanation of the sanskrit word or its historical significance for that and many such words used in this book are perhaps the content of another conversation. I set about reading a great deal of what was on offer about this meditation form and most of the material looked positive and the benefits sounded worth the effort. The technique was very simple in that I had to gaze at a lit candle flame, keeping it at eye level between two and three feet away, as I sat on the floor. The two other things that I was to be conscious of were to first keep my eyes wide open (not blinking the eyelids at all) and closing the eyes the moment they started to water – both sounding like some kind of satvic effort to the ignorant mind. This was at the physical level.

At the mental level, there was also a certain alignment process to be undergone before commencing the 'candle gaze' and after the closure of the eyes. Then there was the spiritual aspect and here is where most of the 'introducers' shared different perspectives on what was to be done. I avoided all such suggestions after trying them out religiously to just stick with witnessing what was unfolding, in silence. The effects of this meditation technique were just plain evident and I will stick to sharing what became apparent at the physical, mental and emotional level and leave out the spiritual part, for the latter is where all the rituals, superstition, blind-faith and confusion begin when one follows concepts – interpretations of the mind that aren't supposed to be verbalised in the first place. 'Be still and know' is perhaps the best applicable statement at that level. At the initial stages, I was gazing for a few minutes and then shutting my eyes as they started to water, but towards the later stages, six or seven months into the technique, I was gazing for a good 20-25 minutes. I began to notice that my concentration on an overall basis increased dramatically; a one-pointedness of the mind, if you will. The eyes were feeling tired immediately but I noticed that my reading glasses were no longer as necessary as they were earlier as my eyesight began to show improvement. This I got cross-checked with a doctor and was mighty pleased with the effort. Lastly, I began to notice a different relationship with fear in that it was diminishing as a felt state.

This then was a great technique but a technique nevertheless. I had in a way got addicted to the process and would find the day a bit listless if I missed a session. That had then become a cause for concern as a new addiction, albeit a satvic one.

A catharsis through dance...5Rhythms as a process

This process, a movement meditation practice devised by Gabrielle Roth, was making the rounds as a great technique to try that was devoid of conversation, superstition and all things associated. It was supposedly one that drew inspiration from many indigenous and world traditions using tenets from a number of esoteric approaches. The core message appealed to me as it purported, 'everything is energy, and moves in waves, patterns and rhythms'. Roth herself, according to what was available online, had described the practice as a soul journey, and had said that by moving the body, releasing the heart, and freeing the mind, one could connect to the essence of the soul, the source of inspiration in which an individual had unlimited possibility and potential.

There were a few centres in London that offered this opportunity, to just dance without a care and dance out different emotional states, through movement. It sounded harmless and the cost too, a mere GBP12 per session, was also not one that hurt the purse. The other huge benefit was that the process involved a high level of aerobic movement – great for the body anyway. Some of Gabrielle's clips on YouTube and on her website were very well presented and appealing. I wasn't sure of the actual modalities or the inner workings that happened as the process got under way but it was worth a try. One of their centres was near my office at Oxford Circus and the event started at around 7:00 p.m. which was perfect timing. My first experience at engaging was one of being conscious of myself and the movements that I was making. Over a period of four weeks that experience shifted to then just being total in the dance, as the dance, and at a mental level it felt very good. However, I was restless for a breakthrough and while this was good as a process, it just did not seem the perfect one for me.

An embryonic experience...immersed in a Floatation Tank

The whole search, according to some of the Masters, is about us wanting to get back to the blissful state we were in when in our mother's womb. It seemed acceptable as a concept for there was also no way of challenging it, by knowing the truth itself. As a part of my travels, I met a lady trainer who was working for an organisation named Avatar whose founder swore by the experiences he had had in a device called the Floatation Tank. This, for those unaware, is a piece of equipment that is shaped like a giant egg and is split horizontally in two halves. The bottom half is filled with a solution of water and salt, the salt so dense in the water that the body floats (as it does in the Dead Sea). The top half is like a giant lid that closes and then one is just left to being immersed in the saltwater solution, in darkness (or with a small light if one wishes), listening to a choice of piped music or just plain silence. The lady suggested I give the Floatation Tank a try and then perhaps join their courses later, as time progressed. The former sat OK with me as the cost of a Floatation Tank experience was about GBP50 while the latter was in the thousands. I was clear that I did not want to waste a penny on rah-rah conversations, or any more mass-hypnosis for all that was just more mental stuff to deal with mental stuff.

Anyway, there was a set-up near Tower Bridge in London that offered a Floatation Tank experience and it seemed like a good thing to try once. I booked a few sessions, diving into the deepest end of the experience by choosing to go with silence and without any lights inside the tank or 'chamber'. This, the experience, was all very well as a means to relax, perhaps similar in a way to having a glass of wine on a calm summer evening, but it wasn't the real thing at all. After the experience, the world outside was the same and the barrage of mental noise and more came back to disturb the inner world. This was an experience like any other experience, but just that. It wasn't one that transcended the senses. I wasn't looking for some kind of balm to deal with what I was going through and so let this go.

Organic food, a raw vegan cuisine, fasting and many a breathing technique...testing the system completely

I was also becoming conscious of what I was eating. The social networks that I was a part of, the meditation camps that I attended and the books that I read were all alive with many opportunities to sample cuisine of a different kind. Most preferred organic raw food (I won't go into the merits and the demerits of organic food over non-organic food here) in the main or at least as close to its original state as possible. There was the opportunity to sample some of that at places like the Vita Organics or Yantra in the City in London, both close to my office on Margaret Street, or 222 in Fulham in the suburbs near my home, and the effect on the body as a whole was amazing. I was a convert the day I started and still practise much of what I have learnt. The body is an amazingly intelligent system, a highly complex one that requires very simple inputs for its maintenance and I was beginning to notice the after-effects of bringing an altered and higher level of consciousness to eating. Fasting too was an option that I had considered as a way to deny the body its basic need – food for survival – and watch that process to the level that was possible.

Cobra breath...another technique, another hope for a breakthrough

While pranayam was the main breathing technique that I practised almost every other day, there was another one called the 'Cobra Breath' that was much spoken of by those in the Tantra circles. I had read a fair bit about what it entailed, the process and its benefits, and was intrigued by the possibilities it offered. There is a Taiwanese teacher by the name of Mantak Chia who has quite a following, who has written many a book and who backed this breathing technique as a means to harnessing sexual energy and transforming it into 'chi' and higher spiritual energies. London's largest bookstore of all things esoteric, Watkins in Soho, has a number of books that threw light on this breathing technique. There was also a great deal of mystery tied to this breathing technique and its genesis. It was rumoured that a great Himalayan yogi by the name of Babaji had offered this as part of a larger Tantra process and that this technique enabled the dormant energy (Shakti) situated at the bottom of the spine to move upwards, changing the electromagnetic properties of the cerebrospinal fluid, allowing for a waking-up state in a higher level of consciousness. All this sounded like jargon to me then but the technique was a simple one and, after a few months of practice, its benefits on overall health and immune system were clearly tangible. It was later in Varanasi that the 'method behind the madness' and a few changes in the process itself were shared with me that it started to make a difference at a level that allowed for a much deeper witnessing state. This, the technique though, isn't one bit necessary and at times can be an excuse to stop the journey itself as the immediate set of experiences can be quite alive and extremely uplifting, offering a 'high' of a very different kind without the side effects normally associated with a drug-induced high.

My visit to the great sage Ramana Maharishi's ashram and later meeting Mooji, another lovely soul who has touched the lives of so many in a meaningful way, made it clear about the direct waking state possibility that made all such practices quite irrelevant. Nevertheless, as a technique it does have potential and under the right tutelage can allow for a number of benefits.

The throttle was at full speed...a blur was all that was visible

At some point in time in the journey I was going through various processes, starting my day at 4:00 a.m. and was committing a good seven to eight hours every day to this search. The trouble was, I still had no idea of what good looked like and in its place was a bunch of concepts, techniques and a hopeful mind. The quantum of knowledge, the currency of many an inane and, at times, an agitated conversation, was growing and so was the distance from everything else. My sleep patterns and overall health were both OK but the body felt far from rested. In fact, it felt restless as if something was amiss and the mind was a bit scattered in its attention. Relationships with those close to me seemed distant and there was an almost complete irrelevance of the NOW, the today and in its place was an expectation of some future state to happen.

My kids must have felt that their father was becoming a new-age hippie but that was far from the truth. I was just 100% engaged in cracking the code of life (if there was one and, knowing what I know now, there isn't one accessible in the way the mind approaches that quest) and yet in spite of all the knowledge (well, as much as was possible over a 17-year period, with the last three being very intense), all the scriptures and the mental and physical gymnastics, I didn't have much to say with deep knowing as my own. I had, in a manner of speaking, become an athlete training for the Olympics but one participating in a dozen events ranging from the marathon run on one hand to a 100 metre sprint on the other, from a welterweight boxing bout on the one hand to an equestrian event on the other.

A breakdown was imminent. With all the circus that had ensued so far, the big question still remained: who was I without my name and fame and without the baggage that appeared mine? I did not have a clue and nothing so far and none of the people I had met pointed me to anything that appealed to my heart as a direct knowing. I was always there and now I had some new baggage, spiritual in its outlook, but baggage nevertheless. That was the real crash and hurt much more than the earlier one. The earlier one was at a physical level and led to an opening. This one was deeper, much deeper and it looked quite dark ahead for there was neither the wisdom to know what to do nor the presence of someone who could show me the way out of the mess I was in. This was a really tough time for everyone close to me. I remember becoming distant and aloof at home, withdrawing contact from old friends and living in a 'semi-comatose' state. My friends then were the squirrels on the heath in Putney, the sparrows and the crow that descended on my apartment in Mumbai and the odd stranger who showed a kind hand.

I was, for all practical purposes, lost to the world and lost to myself. That is how it felt.

BOOK TWO:
The Search, The Breakdown

Chapter 4:
The train to Varanasi: headless and in deep surrender

A one-way ticket...no turning back this time

Until now, the travel to any place and back was time-bound. A return ticket was always in place and if not a return ticket, an open ticket with the option of converting it to one later. Changing plans was never the norm. All the visits so far to meditation camps, to ashrams and more were planned with the objective of going away for a few days and then returning home with whatever benefits the course had to offer. This time it was different. I just did not want to come back to the same old world, safe and secure as it was, as coming back meant living an unanswered question and I was sick of the conundrum.

The pain was just too much, the itch was unbearable, the hurt was just too strong, the 'tamasha' of the marketplace was just plain silly, the need to mould and fall back into a conditioned state was just impossible; take your pick. Too much had changed by then. The possibility of real freedom was always there for I had deep glimpses of that already. There really was no option. I tell you that this is a great state to be in however dire it may sound and perhaps dramatic too; for when it's clear that the past isn't an option, a new world opens up.

I had made arrangements for my family in London, trying to do whatever was possible given the circumstances and converted all assets to cash. Liquidity is great in times of change. The other aspect to handle was my extended family in India and one never really knows what is good enough but I did my best to bring safety and certainty to those who were dependent on me. It wasn't a big deal for me for I wasn't in the least identifying with my possessions but the process was painful. It brought up a lot of emotional angst between me and my wife and then me and my mother. My mother was at loss to understand what this, my journey, was all about. It was all very well to see a film on celluloid about some crazy seeker but this was in real life, in her own family. She had set aside her life to provide for me and my sisters and to finally see me through the IIT and the

IIM (engineering and business schools in India and perhaps amongst the very best) to now perhaps see all her efforts turn to dust. She was a bit distraught; her prayer time almost doubled overnight, but my sister Yogita was very supportive of my journey. It isn't that she knew what was to follow but she loved me so much that she just trusted what I was on. Her stance was simple and she said that I had to follow my intuition and I should be allowed to go.

I booked a one-way train ticket to Varanasi, the 'city of light', as it is known. I have no idea why I chose Varanasi but it just felt right going there. It was, in scriptures, the place supposedly beyond the three worlds – in effect, the three states of waking, sleeping and dreaming. There are other interpretations, but for the sake of a sane conversation I will stick to this otherwise it gets into some really esoteric realms and it is pointless having a discussion or dialogue about such things. This was a city I had lived in way back in 1983 for four years as a part of my engineering studies but had not connected to it in a way that allowed for fond memories, other than those in the campus where we students lived. Then the only thing that caught the eye was the overflowing dirt and filth that seemed to be flooding the city.

I did not want anything but was completely open to what was offered as a gift. I realised that aspects related to travel, hotel stay and food at some level were distractions and too much planning of such issues created a set of expectations that itself got in the way of experiencing the now. Birds when they migrate don't really plan to settle on some specific perch or eat a particular worm, nor do they fly over a certain path. They are just guided by an inner intelligence and they go with that, unafraid and in sheer abandon. I too had given up wanting to plan and prepare for the inconsequentials and just wanted to enjoy, be a witness to the journey. Even this statement is partially true, for I really did not know what I was getting into and what I was going to find. I just wanted to head to Varanasi and that was it.

The train to Varanasi...a 30 hour expanse in time but much more in sheer silence

I was travelling in very different fashion: by train, with a backpack, a few clothes, some dry fruits, a cutting knife, a bottle of water and some fruits. This train journey was one I had not taken for a long time but it felt right for once, being on a train; there was nothing to do but just surrender to its timing and that felt like a huge relief. Before leaving home, I had prepared a very simple meal, listened to some quiet music on the iPod and was waiting for the cab to arrive. The cab service was prompt in picking me up from my apartment; the cab driver was a talkative but well-meaning guy who had migrated to Mumbai from Ayodhya, the birthplace of the legendary or mythical figure Ram. He spoke about his life, his kids and how blessed he felt to be able to be a responsible father and a law-abiding citizen of the country. Our conversations were easy paced and I shared with him a few things about my past, my search and more. A call from my sister Yogita just before I was to reach the station allowed for an even calmer state to descend and I experienced deep love and support from her at one of the most testing moments of my life.

00:10 a.m. at the CST (erstwhile VT Station, the central terminus for trains leaving Mumbai) was when the famed Mahanagari Express was to leave for Varanasi and the crowd at the station was a good 1,500-2,000+, North Indians from the states of UP and Bihar mostly, waiting for the train to dock on the platform. I saw a huge queue of guys, perhaps 300 or more with bags of all kinds, waiting patiently in front of a uniformed policeman. These guys were the ones travelling unreserved. I had the privilege of having my ticket booked by an agent and emailed to me and my bogie was a good ten-minute walk from the start of the station entrance. I walked into the bogie and set about searching for my berth which turned out to be an upper one. I shared the compartment space with a Mr & Mrs Dhoot, a middle-aged couple heading to Varanasi to attend a relative's marriage and a Mr Chaturvedi, a railway officer heading for a new posting in the north.

The journey began at midnight, the train leaving Mumbai in the middle of the night and by the time we were an hour into the journey, most had settled down to sleep. I was on the top berth, dressed in black-coloured, loose cotton trousers and a grey long-sleeved T-shirt. The body was tired after being awake for almost 18 hours and the mind was tired from perhaps a three year sojourn. Sleep was a natural reliever from the 'always on' state and I must have drifted into a silent state in about 15-20 minutes of my head touching the pillow. I was woken up by the commotion in the gangway; some local railway catering bloke taking orders for lunch! It was 8:00 a.m. and I thought it was too early to contemplate lunch but that is how it was, for the guy was cutting competition out of the equation by beginning early. The dreaded disease, a life driven by fear, was making its presence felt here too and I was impressed with his single-minded devotedness to his work. That was followed by tea-sellers offering hot tea to those who had woken up. I did not risk my system with tea that early in the journey and just managed to get myself a bottle of mineral water. Oranges taste divine at breakfast, especially so if there is nothing else on offer and so it was that way; I ate two of the oranges I had brought along with me from Mumbai. Sitting on the upper deck has its privileges and problems. I had my own safe haven six feet above the floor and away from the marketplace that was the compartment but the flip side was that I had no freedom on when to come down and take a seat downstairs. That was decided by the guys sleeping below (Mr Chaturvedi in this case) and my travel mate seemed to like the night better than the morning sun. It was already 10:00 a.m. and I was still sitting on the top berth, waiting for the man to wake up and allow me to get some sun and some fresh air.

Indian train junctions – places where trains take a break to shift routes, add more bogies and the like – have a life of their own.

We had reached a city in the afternoon on the way by the name of Itarsi – a junction and a halting place for a change of engines perhaps and a welcome hot meal for the hungry passengers. I was having a short walk on the platform when I saw four other trains amble up and take their positions on some of the other vacant platforms. The train adjoining ours was leaving the platform, heading back to Mumbai, and looked like a slow train from the quality of the bogies and the lack of any first-class options. A mass of people arriving, a mass leaving and many more already at the junction; a feeding frenzy starting with every train's arrival at the platform. Although there was much chaos, it also sounded melodious in a way that I can't describe and the only difference that I noticed was that I was not resisting anything. In the midst of all the chaos, I saw a young family of four squatting on the platform, perhaps waiting for their train journey to begin that might be a few days away. The two young children looked like they were living rough, malnourished and in need of some food and I walked up to one of the stalls to pick up a dish and a sweet for them. What struck me as beautiful was when I gave the packet to the little girl, she walked back to her father and handed the entire tray to him, who then looked at its contents and gave the sweet back to her and her brother first and waited for them to finish. That felt like a beautiful expression of parental love, the economic class notwithstanding.

The chaos outside on the platform was nicely balanced by the silence within the air conditioned train compartment, as passengers were quickly darting out and back in with their purchases. The silence was broken by the odd tea-seller wanting to attract attention but the sales pitch was muted. This was, as I know and experienced then too, the perfect occasion for people to break the ice and offer tea to their co-travellers and begin many an informal conversation. Compare this with, say, a travel from London to Paris or Brussels by Eurostar: guys reading The Economist or The Independent, some listening to their iPods and sipping perhaps black tea or coffee and you can well imagine the 'party atmosphere' that builds up in trains in India. By the time it was late afternoon, the guys around (Mr Dhoot and Mr Chaturvedi) had gleaned so much information about me and about each other that I am sure someone listening would have had enough to complete a horoscope or, better still, a complete profile of any of us. A pseudo-family bond was being formed and it felt harmless. Luckily I wasn't single, so no marriage proposal was brought forward, although I have had that experience too, many years ago on the way to Pune from Mumbai.

A few seats away, a Muslim family had made themselves comfortable on the two berths that were allocated to them but they had four children in all and so the kids were quietly grabbing space wherever they could. They looked a tough lot and the father looked like one too; a youngish, in his late 20s guy who was working with some mobile company (I heard him share that with someone else on the phone and he was talking so loudly that even the rattle of the train was not a hindrance to hearing the dialogue. Perhaps he wanted to speak above the 85-90 decibel level anyway). The next compartment had a devout Muslim, a kind sort of gent, very genial and accommodating, who was reading an Urdu paper and sharing its contents with his co-passengers. At the entrance of the compartment was a family, a portly middle-aged man, his wife, three daughters and a son and they were going back for a holiday it seemed. They had probably the biggest in-house food store in the entire train that made its way to the plates they kept ready for use whenever a train reached a platform. The aroma was a mixed one but, in the end, the only thing I could smell was the spices that were used. The food looked far from being nutritious: oily and extreme in taste (a chilli on each plate and a sweet too, a garlic paste to add to that mix that we could all smell) and the colour in the main was a predominant brown with shades of yellow and a few red patches. There was no green, no water (tea instead and sugar, too) and it all looked extremely unhealthy to me. The man and his wife looked like they needed a health check-up and a complete overhaul but their eyes were still young and they seemed to exude so much love towards their children that it was a nice sight to see. It seemed like the whole of India was represented in some form or the other in the train and that felt good too.

The landscape outside was a constantly changing one; nothing standardised (the beauty and yet the bane in India) but just clumps of grass, the odd bullock cart carrying bales of hay, women carrying firewood, children playing near a river, small villages and towns with a predominant brick-red colour to their homes and a raft of banners spread between roads and adverts painted on walls that marketed goods from food mixers to televisions to condoms to fertilizers. Just looking at this stationary circus was a lovely experience as I was transported to my childhood, remembering the time when there was an entertainment equipment called a 'bioscope' where the guy who brought it along asked us kids to kneel down, cup our hands around our eyes and watch the 'mini movie' that the bioscope was about to show. For those who don't know what such an instrument looks like, please do a search on Google Images and see for yourself. For those who know and have had the experience, I am sure that just the remembrance would have brought a smile to your lips by now.

By now, Mr Chaturvedi was giving an elaborate treatise to the Dhoots on-train scheduling, the towns and villages that our train would arrive at and stuff about many other train routes. Mrs Dhoot was the silent type, always looking out of the window or at the floor but never directly at Mr Chaturvedi, who himself was conscious that the dialogue, or monologue rather, was directed at Mr Dhoot. I was amazed at his local knowledge but was hoping they'd jump to something more entertaining, something that I could add to or at least reference to my own life. I noticed my own disinterest in the conversation that I was hearing and then witnessed that, at that moment of noticing, something else started to unfold. I started to notice simple things and the beauty of how it all was, all at the same time: the kids on the adjoining berths who had now taken to swinging from one top berth to the other; someone's radio was belting an old classic; Mr Dhoot's way of asking leading questions; and Mrs Dhoot's yellow-green saree with some really intricate embroidery work. Mrs Dhoot later climbed on to the top berth and started reciting a prayer meant to appease the monkey god Hanuman, one that was recited to ward off evil and attract strength. Mr Dhoot had set the scene for a light afternoon nap that was to extend until dinner time as I saw it and Mr Chaturvedi was staring out and seemed at peace. My temporary train family had expanded and it felt good for no reason.

We all settled into a quiet phase of the journey; me on the top berth with my thoughts, my little book and a pen and the others on their berths. Dinner time was a quiet one as the Dhoots opened the home-made tiffins they had brought along, Mr Chaturvedi with the lunch he ordered and I with a sparse diet of a few oranges, a banana and some almonds. The night slowly drifted in; the lights were turned off by Mr Chaturvedi (he was taking the lead at all such things and I was saved of the chaperoning as I was on the top berth, in a quiet cocoon of my own) and used the small night-lamp to make observations about what was cooking, what was surfacing up on my mind and what I was feeling about all that. It all seemed very peaceful and, in that state, I switched off the lamp to allow for a state of deeper rest. I was woken up by the sound of someone moving about and realised it was very early morning, 4:00 a.m. or so, and Varanasi would be in view any moment. As I looked outside the window, the train was crossing the River Ganges; the ghats lit, a few boats in the waters and the train moving at a very slow speed. If I had been in a second-class compartment, without air-conditioning but with open windows, I would have heard the clinking of coins as the faithful ones threw them into the Ganges and wished for good tidings. This time it was all in silence. No one spoke much but as the platform arrived we just exchanged glances of gratitude and of completion; we had arrived here safely and the next leg of the journey was about to commence separately. I would never see them again but in some unusual way I still carry them as qualities within me, their conversations and subtle nuances still alive and fresh in memory.

Travelling one way, without a return ticket and without a planned agenda, had its advantages, real advantages. For the first time, little things started to look beautiful, those that I would have missed completely. My entire life story and all the baggage with that, for the few moments that seemed like hours had just disappeared, and in its place was just a state of deep silence. It was no big deal but considering what I was going through, knowing what had been on my mind for the past few years and perhaps more, this state was a blessing and, what is more, it required no effort at all other than a silent, undiluted attention. The beauty of the moment, the sensitivity to the NOW, was incredible and I saw and felt deeply that I could step in and influence it too, just by what I paid attention to.

Imagine being drunk on air and water, totally intoxicated; that is how it felt.

BOOK TWO:
The Search, The Breakdown

Chapter 5:
The silent vigil, grace, melody: Manikarnika Ghat, my Teacher, the Kirtan

Varanasi, the city of light...an enigma for some, a homecoming for the others

Just beginning this chapter, with my attention on this part of the journey itself, allows for such a calm feeling to unfold. Varanasi is Varanasi – unlike any other place on the planet for it is a city where rank polarities are juxtaposed. Abject poverty and unbelievable opulence, birth and death, sublime beauty and sheer filth, the wisdom of the ages and the rank darkness of the mind; this stark polarity is a shock for most, for our lives are lived in a cocooned manner. The beautiful and the useful are kept in close vicinity while all that is dirty is managed away from our daily gaze. Living such a 'cocooned' life as a society has its side effects in that, as a people, we bring that attitude to all aspects of our lives and 'separation' as a process then has commenced at a deeply unconscious level for most. Varanasi in a way is a deeply tantric city for it celebrates death while its direct opposite, Khajuraho, celebrates life. The real privilege a city like Varanasi provides, or for that matter any place in the world really, is to be a witness to what is on show, rank polarities without being affected by either. Seeing all that is, hope and despair or birth and death as one continuum without having to side with one or the other; recognising the mechanics of the mind and the misery it creates by such choices is itself the waking up that allows for freedom.

Anyway, back to my journey and the moment-to-moment unfolding of ordinary miracles that was to follow. The air outside was crisp and cold; the mercury touches single digits in December in Varanasi and the time on my watch was nearing 5:00 a.m. The sun had yet to make its way to shed light on this city but the lights from the platform and station were enough to allow me to walk, backpack and a bottle of water in my hand, towards the exit. As I neared the exit, I saw, as is the case with most Indian stations, hordes of passengers sleeping on the outside of the platform, perhaps having come early, possibly the previous night, to board the train that was to leave in the morning. A tea-seller was making his way quietly about the sleeping crowd and getting on with his business. An army of rickshaw drivers descended upon the passengers, asking for business and offering deals. I was including everything and rejecting nothing, not wanting to make any move at all, no effort other than just witnessing what was going on. I stood quietly for a short while outside the station exit, breathing in the sights and sounds, looking at the dark grey sky that was slowly turning colour at its edges. I had no place to stay, no agenda planned but was just fully, 100% ready for whatever showed up as a gift, trusting that it was meant for me. In fact, I was even beyond this 'it's meant for me' mindset. I was just glad to be alive and everything else after that was a bonus.

Making my way around...being led rather than leading

A slightly short and stocky guy with perhaps a two-day old beard walked up to me and just picked up my backpack that was on the floor and asked me to come to his rickshaw. I looked into his eyes and smiled, following him to his vehicle. This was a first of sorts for me in my life, trusting a stranger, as neither had he asked me where I was going, nor had we agreed any price. We walked in silence and he dumped my backpack behind the passenger seat and I sat in, holding my small shoulder bag that had all my possessions. Before I could suggest anything, he asked if I wanted to have a cup of tea, to which I replied in the affirmative. He led me out of the station precincts to a tea stall a few yards away across the road and walked out to order tea, asking me to stay in his vehicle while he managed the process. By the time the tea arrived, I had taken out a small pack of biscuits, dipping them into the hot tea (this was some special tea I heard him ordering, which included extra milk and some cardamom) and sharing a few with him. We finished the tea ceremony in silence and it felt really good. He then asked me where I was wanting to go, to which I replied that I had not booked a hotel yet but was a former student at the university in Varanasi and would prefer to go to my old campus and check for a place through the students' alumni association at one of the many lovely guest houses in the sprawling campus. The trouble was, that part of the world woke up very late and office bearers would make it to their desks after 10:00 a.m. and then head out for one of the many longish tea ceremonies. The only thing under my control was my ability to wait and so I asked him for a quote for being my driver for the entire day. A fee of USD14 was what he felt was right for his services and I agreed immediately. I then shared why I was in Varanasi, couching my language with words that he would relate to and said that I was back to pay my respects to the city and the energy that was alive within. I mentioned I wanted to visit one of the leading Aghori ashrams in the city or its neighbourhood, a few ghats, the university campus and a few other places. He suggested that we could sit on the banks of the Ganges till it became daybreak and then make our way to each of the places that I spoke about. I had no pre-planned idea of what I would do at each of the places but it was just OK to set out a marker on the places I could sample and then move on. It was also clear to me that while I had made an impromptu list, many a new place would get added as the day progressed. With that simple exchange of expectations and an exchange of our mobile numbers, we set out.

This step, the next, the one after that and so on...an experience in conscious living

I had lived in Varanasi a good 25 years ago but had never really felt the city, felt its energy and what it truly had to offer. I had never listened to her with an open heart. Until then, the idea was just to use the city, or any place for that matter, as a waiting room before boarding the train for the next leg of the journey to some illusory destination. That attitude, deeply unconscious and yet symbolic, was perhaps one that manifested across all aspects of my life, or so it seemed. So many friends, relatives and yet the connection was one in a state of 'travel'; I had not really stopped all thoughts and listened with my heart to any perhaps – and neither did they, for the only connections I remembered deeply (the heart on song) were with my late grandmother and my sister Yogita. There surely were moments of that kind with many a friend or close relative or a sport but the melody was always short-lived. This, I realised, was such a tragedy, such an opportunity missed, to be in the moment and just be a witness to what was unfolding. The attention, almost always, was on the past or the future and the miracle, the beauty and the innocence of the present was sacrificed instead.

This time in Varanasi it felt different. Without a place to stay, without a planned agenda and without the rush to get any place, I was just watching everything and it seemed as though I was doing so with a fresh pair of eyes. Although the journey had begun, time seemed to slow down in ways not experienced before. It was still very early, 5:30 a.m. or so, and Ramcharan (the driver's name) suggested we head to Assi Ghat, one that was just newly done-up and offered a good place to just sit in silence for it was away from the other busy ghats. I just nodded and off we went, the rickshaw making its way along the narrow corridors of the city, which within a few hours would get completely packed with traffic coming from all directions. As we drove along, Ramcharan started to hum some tune that did not seem like one from the films but a local one. Halfway through the journey, he slowed down the rickshaw and gestured with his hand and said that we were approaching an Aghor ashram and would I be interested in having a look. It was still dark and knowing that sunrise was still another half an hour or so away, I took that up and had him stop the rickshaw at the gates of this ashram. For those uninitiated in the mystic arts, especially Tantra, there are two paths to witnessing the mind. The first is following the mind's desires, its attachments, which is what I had been trained in over the past few years. The other is watching its aversions. Aghori vidya, at a very basic level, is a tantric practice that is purported to enable a transcendence of the mind through the process of witnessing its aversions. There are a million rumours, beliefs and superstitions about this art form, the miracles it is supposed to allow and more but I won't go into any of that for it wasn't the subject of my search. I just wanted to know who I was and to get freedom from the 'programmed' way that I was living my life; an interest in miracles and all things esoteric had long faded away for I had realised the pointlessness of that quest. There are many books on the Aghor path but most spend a huge amount of time on the 'miracles and cures' offered by the path rather than something more sublime: freedom itself. I sensed that freedom is such a vague concept and that today it's taken for granted but at a very gross level. The bondage to conditioning, to societal norms, to body desires and mental afflictions is subtle and not understood. With that, freedom in its truest sense is totally missed. Not many really understand their life in such terms.

The Kinaram Baba Ashram...as big as it gets in its league

The rickshaw stopped at the gates and there were a few souls sitting at the entrance who seemed to be engrossed in a silent conversation. I noticed that the ashram gate was adorned with huge replicas of the human skull. The ashram complex looked dark as the lights were switched off but had a peaceful look about it. The man at the gate was an old gent, perhaps in his late 50s, and was courteous in welcoming me to the place but refused to divulge what the ashram was all about. He invited me to a prayer that was held every evening at 7:00 p.m. and said I could come a bit earlier and get to see and know the place. He wasn't the least bit interested in getting money out of me and that struck me as a different state of being. The experience at many a temple or its precincts is one of being harangued for money with the promise of some deity appeasement and a set of rituals for that. The man also looked very calm and measured in his demeanour. I bade him goodbye and left for Assi Ghat, mentioning that I would be back the same evening. In fact, it would be three days before I would cross the road this ashram was on.

Assi Ghat...a place transfixed in time, meeting angels with large hearts

This was a small ghat when compared to the other big ones along the banks of the Ganges but the local establishment had spent a great deal of money in its modernisation (as is possible in a place like Varanasi). In the early 1980s this did not even figure on the traveller circuit but by now had become hugely popular. Many an Israeli tourist is now seen on this ghat as some of the local hotels began catering to their needs and this ghat has now become a hub for that community. We reached the banks of the Ganges by around 6:30 a.m. and the early rays of dawn could be seen on the horizon.

I left my bags in the rickshaw and walked to the edge of the banks, sitting on one of the many steps that have been newly-created for pilgrims to sit on, bathe themselves and perhaps worship the Ganges. I was silent and just watching everything; everything. It was a heavy moment that I can't describe accurately in words but it felt as though I had come to a huge watershed in my life. It did feel that way and it felt, to be honest, quite hopeless. My life as a Goldman's investment banker was over, the business that I was managing as an entrepreneur was not appealing, my relationships at home and outside looked out of sync with where I was, my trysts with all things spiritual had given me a million skills and powers but there really was no peace in my heart; I just felt I was living the life of a ghost and the only person on this planet with whom I was truly in touch was my sister Yogita. I then looked at the rising sun and decided to go through one of the many morning rituals, sun gazing, and set up the posture and the focus to begin the process. Somewhere midway, I don't know how and why, I began to cry, tears rolling down from my eyes and over my cheeks and I knew the time had come to concede a complete defeat. I looked at the sun and in silent deference acknowledged that I had lost, was still lost and had no clue of anything in the world and that I needed help and was willing to do whatever it took to just get a good night's sleep. This went on for some time and the early hours of the morning allowed for a very nurturing space around; the ghat was sparsely filled with people and the ones who were making the rounds of the place were merchants who were setting their stalls for the day. From the corner of my eye, I saw a flower- and incense-selling lady, setting her stall but also feeding a calf that had wandered to her set-up, in search of food. I saw her pick out some flowers from her basket and offer them to the calf.

Slowly, I made my way to her stall, an open-air set up, almost a square platform that was raised about two feet in height, installed on four massive boulders, and she sat in the middle with her wares in front. There was a child sitting next to her who looked like her son and who offered me a namaste as I stood in front of them. I asked her about the ritual and what it entailed by way of cost and process and she explained that I needed a Brahmin priest to conduct a prayer for me and that she could provide the ingredients: a few incense sticks, a flower garland, a few flowers and leaves and a wick that was soaked in clarified butter (that is what is expected but, given the economic climate and the need to be competitive, normal oil has replaced clarified butter) that was to be lit and 'let go' in the Ganges. I wasn't one bit interested in asking a Brahmin priest for his services and instead asked her to be my 'priest' for the morning prayer and the look on her face suggested that this was a first for her too. She slowly walked with me and, at the edge of the river, suggested I recite a few prayers and joined me in chanting what was a simple prayer in every way.

We walked back in silence and, on reaching her stall, I realised that I had no loose change to pay for her goods. I suggested that she keep the Rs100 (approximately USD2) and then return the change when I visited the ghat again but she suggested that I pay her the next time I visited the place. This was another first of sorts for me, for in a way what she was risking was perhaps her profit from a whole day's effort and she was not in the least perturbed by that. The child who was with her was her son who was doing duty before heading for school. The sight of a working mother and her child and the experience I had, of just trust without cause, was an immensely beautiful one. I walked back to the rickshaw; Ramcharan had picked up a local paper and was happily sitting on the back seat, legs raised on the bar in front and engaged in a silent dialogue with the paper. After rummaging through the backpack, I found a packet of biscuits and some oranges that I carried back to the flower-seller's son. On my way back to the parking lot, I realised it was 9:00 a.m.; a great deal of time had passed but Ramcharan was still waiting. He could easily have vanished with my bags and made enough by selling the goods (my phones, wallet, passport and more) to buy another rickshaw. That was another first for me – trusting a complete stranger when my entire life was about protecting myself from being cheated by those unknown to me. Here was one Ramcharan who I did not know a few hours ago but who now was taking care of my belongings and my well-being for no reason, the service contract between us notwithstanding. I was later to visit Assi Ghat again for another memorable set of moments that took me to another world; the saying 'same planet, different worlds' became so, so real for me then.

Campus accommodation at the LDH (Lakshman Das Guest House)...
bless the founder, the great late Madan Mohan Malviya

The ride from Assi Ghat to the campus was a quick one but we stopped at a place midway called Lanka for breakfast: an oily, nutrition-poor but cholesterol-rich serving of puris (hollow fried Indian bread is the closest that I can describe it as) and a vegetable made of potatoes and soya which had a layer of oil on top that looked like automotive grease. My 'UK stomach' was to get a ride on the wild side and with my intention of not resisting anything, I just tucked into the fare that was offered. Ramcharan was happily eating what was on his plate and regaling me with stories about his life, about Varanasi too, but still keeping a distance, an air of formality in our conversations. Beyond the 'greasy hands/slight stubble/rough clothes' was a man who was a father, a son, a husband and beyond, or rather before that, a human being with desires and aspirations. He seemed happy for the most part and his view was that if he could manage a good night's sleep, he considered himself blessed. I loved his simplicity and his direct nature and our conversations became interspersed with moments where he would mouth a sentence or two on 'life' and what it took to creating a wholesome life – stuff that belied his economic background. He was, he mentioned, just working to get his kids through college and after that he would retire with his wife to their village.

We crossed Lanka and the statue of the founder that is so beautifully installed at the entrance of the campus. With closed eyes and a silent prayer, I bowed down to the founder and the spirit he so epitomised and asked for his guidance in this journey of mine. I felt deeply that I had not lived up to the ideals of the institution he had established but was back again at the gates of the campus, with an open heart and wanting to start from scratch. For those who don't know, the late Madan Mohan Malviya was a legendary figure in the days before independence, a freedom fighter notable for his role in the Indian Independence movement and was one of the leading lights in the Indian National Congress alongside the late Mahatma Gandhi. I wasn't the least bit interested in his role at the country level but greatly admired the fact that when he built the university campus on funds raised from charity, he ensured that neither he nor any of his family members or friends benefited from the effort, immediately or over time. He was a real example of selfless service and in my state of looking at all things afresh, this seemed like a noble quality to honour and his spirit a fitting one to pay respects to. I asked for his guidance and support in this deep, dark hour of mine for I was truly lost and there was no one I could pick up the phone and speak to.

The conversations before leaving Mumbai with the institute guest house co-ordinator weren't helpful as he was in and out of the local hospital and not in a mood to give my need for accommodation at the alumni guest house any attention. Rather than push him for help, I had just let it be. On reaching the campus gate, we made our way to the guest house and explored options for staying in one of the rooms. December is 'marriage season' in India so it was impossible to get a place to stay within the campus but the co-ordinator had managed to speak to a different guest house. The university has over seven of them but all were overflowing with guests from conventions that were being held at various places in the campus; however, one could manage a bed for me for a few nights. I made my way to the famed Lakshman Das Guest House (LDH as it's referred to in the campus) to meet the caretaker, a devout and saintly-looking South Indian who wore a beaded necklace around his neck with clothes to match. The only accommodation that was available was shared, in a dormitory with three beds in a room, but I was lucky to have the entire room to myself.

The guesthouse was surrounded by trees and it all felt very safe and secure. The photographs of former teachers and office bearers who had played an important role in making the university what it was adorned the walls at the entrance and the dining hall too. My eyes were always drawn to the late founder's photograph on the wall; our silent conversation was a regular feature with me in deep gratitude for the gift that he had made available and seeking his blessings for what was to unfold. The guest house was done up in a style reminiscent of the 1950s: staff wearing starched-white cottons; dining hall cutlery made of heavy silver, although I wonder if it was real silver; and the telephones in the room, perhaps analogue. The room I was staying in was sparse but very clean and silent and it felt good to stay at such a location rather than in the city in a hotel. After a light lunch, I set out with Ramcharan to see the main ghats, especially Dashashwamedh in Godowlia.

Harischandra Ghat...raging fires and yet a sombre silence

On the way to the ghat we passed another landmark ghat called Harischandra Ghat, famed for the story attached to its legacy. I won't go into that story here but it's one worth reading and you could look up Google or Wikipedia and know for yourself. The late Mahatma Gandhi was deeply influenced by the story of Raja (King) Harischandra himself. Anyway, this was a burning ghat; Varanasi had two burning ghats of which this was one. The other was up north called Manikarnika Ghat. The former is one that is used by the masses for cremating the dead while the latter is chosen by the more elite. Their pricing reflects the positioning as well as the fact that they also have very interesting and very different legacies. Ramcharan suggested we look at a hotel that he knew offered a good deal and I followed his advice and allowed myself to be guided. The hotel was a strange one, a really strange one in that the courtyard at the entrance of the hotel was half used as a storing ground for logs of wood, those used for the cremation grounds (Hindus burn the dead as you know) at the ghat ahead. The room that I was shown was a simple one, devoid of even the most basic of luxuries, and it seemed to me that this was perhaps used as a resting place by the relatives of the dead, those who came to see the dead bodies off at the ghat. The smell of burning flesh too was a clear reminder of the proximity of the cremation grounds but there really wasn't any violent or revulsive reaction from me. I actually felt like walking to the cremation ground myself, which was perhaps a minute's walk away. As I made my way with Ramcharan to the site, the first thing that struck me was the sound of crackling wood and the dance of the fire above the three sites that were currently being used. Indian cremation grounds are sombre places, not for the faint-hearted, and although as a part of my earlier stay in Varanasi way back in the mid 1980s I did see the two ghats, the look was always a cursory one; death was a taboo, an unknown entity to be scared of and the ghats signified that. The air of gloom, the sorrow expressed by the relatives and the sight of human flesh burning in the fire was just too much for my senses then. Perhaps it is this way for most people in India. This time I was beyond wanting to run away or looking for a diversion; my senses were anyway not attracted to anything in particular. They were just in the NOW or so it felt, for the silence was of a very, very different quality. I stood watching the spectacle and I use that word with the greatest of deference for those suffering, those working there, to the venue and to all that was there. As I watched and watched, I started to feel and become aware of a few things: the fire on each of the sites was alive and a dance of sorts was underway, very similar to the music experience I had in Bhagsu with the difference that the melody here was a sombre one. The other thing I noticed was that I started to see beauty in what was a really macabre sight for most. I wasn't really making any mental notes or wanting to turn away but was witnessing what was and it seemed deeply peaceful. One of the sites closest to me was by now witnessing some effort by those working there as the fire needed attention and the corpse needed a shift in its position to get maximum heat from the fire. That was another moment when something else within me started to unfold: an insight perhaps or a message, but a blessing nevertheless. The corpse was being pronged with two short bamboo poles by the workers, almost a barbeque scene of sorts, but their lack of emotion and the sight of the mortal remains being twisted, turned and pushed made me realise the futility of many a desire (the skin on the face and skull of the corpse was by now burning and was turning brown and black) that the one who had departed would have had and, indeed, the pointlessness of my own desires. That was a huge realisation and I felt an even deeper silence descend at that very moment. Ramcharan was seeing all this from a distance and he walked up to me and asked me if I wanted to move on. We left Harischandra Ghat soon after; I realised that we were at that venue for over two hours but it must have seemed like a whole day.

Manikarnika Ghat.. timeless, consuming all that is the 'Past'

This experience of the cremation grounds on the banks of the Ganges wasn't a planned one and I felt then that there still was some unfinished business for me at the ghats and I intuitively asked Ramcharan to head to the larger of the two cremation grounds, the Manikarnika Ghat. What was to follow altered my life in ways that I can't completely describe. It just isn't possible to verbalise it for words fall short.

This is one of the top three ghats on the Ganges in Varanasi and many a Japanese tourist, and all those who visit the city and pay the river a visit, can be seen staring at the sight of the burning bodies, taking photographs or listening to what the local guide has to share. The entrance to the ghat from the city is through really narrow lanes, no more than three or four feet in width at some places, the sides of which are packed with shops of all kinds: books, food, groceries, spices and condiments, a pharmacy and so on. It's almost as if there is an air of self-sufficiency to that place. The buzz in the lanes is regularly broken by the chants of 'Ram naam satya hai' (the name of Ram is truth) by the relatives of the dead, as the bodies, placed on bamboo stretchers and tied with red cloth and golden twine, are carried on shoulders to the cremation grounds. Nothing really affects business in the lanes and there isn't even a momentary pause by those transacting. The guy sipping tea would continue with his indulgence and the guy selling groceries would continue with his duties; that is how it is and rather than see it as a sign of callousness, it's just that the locals are used to seeing such a sight (a dead body) and their mark of respect is perhaps expressed in a moment's silence that only they know and are deeply comfortable with. The entrance or view of the ghat from the river is a bit different as it has all the makings of a Sir David Attenborough movie with all the colour, the drama, the contrasts and the historical skyline or silhouette of the city as a backdrop. Tourists in search of a quick round-up prefer the latter route, as can be expected, but

Ramcharan wanted to drop me off at the nearest entry point to the ghat from the city side and that settled the issue of access.

I started my slow walk along one of the main entry lanes to the ghat and was struck by the aroma of fresh tea being brewed at one of the stalls. My shoulder bag contained a hand sanitiser that was handy at such a place and I stopped for my cuppa only to stare at another store across the way that sold a wide range of savouries, Indian snacks and sweets that ranged from the deep-fried spicy to the ice-cooled sugary. I label such fare 'vegetarian junk food' that is far from healthy but just stimulates the inner linings of the stomach and intestines for a lot of work but no gain; more on this later in the chapter on a rediscovery of total well-being. My eyes settled on a combo-snack suggested by the owner himself, which started with a spicy, deep-fried dish accompanied by some fiery sauce and followed with a really sugary sweet made of curdled milk, all this interlaced with sips of the tea that the stall next door had provided. This kind of diet is a toxic one but this was way back in 2009 and I wasn't yet awake to the possibility of total well-being, starting with a sound physical state. Food anyway wasn't a priority then and so it was; the stuff tucked in and I walked the narrow by-lanes, asking those around for directions to the main ghat. It did not last long though, my search for the right direction to the cremation grounds, for I saw and heard a funeral procession pass by and from then on all I had to do was to follow the trail: flowers strewn on the lanes, the smell of burning incense and fallen ash at sporadic intervals.

The sight of the ghats for the first time, from the inside out, was an amazing one. Imagine visiting a beach during sunset and imagine seeing the beach from a boat, not looking at the setting sun but at the beach itself. That is how it felt; I felt I was a part of the ghat and the onlookers, the tourists were on boats in the river, busy taking photographs and the like. I walked down the steps of the ghat and it was a sight to see: the filth of animal excrement; the stench of burning human flesh; cows and goats eating the discarded flowers from the dead bodies or even grazing on those that adorned the bodies waiting in a queue to be burnt; dogs looking hungrily and in hope perhaps of landing a piece of flesh and bone; relatives of those departed waiting patiently for their turn to offer the mortal remains to one of the sites; and finally the sight of almost nine burning pyres. This, to me, was not a sight to click pictures of, but one to sit and witness what was and I felt like walking to a perch and watching all that I could from there. It was then, at that very moment, that I felt I had to spend time at this ghat and made a mental note to visit the place again. I was in the city for many days and visited Manikarnika every day, sometimes twice in a day, and would sit (stand rather) for hours at a stretch, just witnessing what was unfolding. I left the ghat after a while; Ramcharan was waiting as patiently as ever to take me back to the guest house for the night. We agreed to meet again in the morning for another round of visits in the city.

Ordinary miracles, unconditional love and more...the magic had begun

We reached the guesthouse quite late at night, 10:00 p.m. or so. As it wasn't a typical commercial set-up that offered round-the-clock room service, it seemed as though I was going to have to sleep on an empty stomach, which, considering how the day had begun and progressed, wasn't such a bad thing. I learnt from the shift-in-charge that the kitchen was closed for the night but I could perhaps walk in and pick up a jug of water for the night. This too was acceptable for it involved no effort and the mind wasn't complaining. The stock of dry fruits that I had brought along gave me the comfort that a half-full gas tank does on a long journey. The pangs of hunger were very much there but so was a relaxed state of witnessing that hunger and the changes that were taking place in my body.

I walked quietly to the dining hall, opened the main door that opened into it from the passage and looked for the light switch to turn on. It was dark inside but after a few guesses I managed to find it and turn it on. As I was walking back, jug in hand, I heard someone politely ask for me, not by name but in a way that made me stop. I turned back to see an oldish man who ideally should have retired by now going by his looks (the balding pate and a mighty tired frame), but his eyes exuded a warmth that was very different and so did his voice. He wanted to know if I had had dinner and, on knowing that I hadn't, mentioned that he had seen me check in that morning and knew that I had had a long day with a very early start. He then offered to cook a quick meal for me but requested me to accompany him to the kitchen as turning on the lights of the dining hall and serving food again at this time of the night was against the rules. In the quiet of the kitchen, he was still the boss and, what is more, he and his colleagues had yet to commence their meals. I was really surprised by this gesture, deeply touched to say the least, and walked with him without uttering a word. I sat in silence as he rustled up a quick and mighty delicious meal for me that I relished with my heart. Every morsel tasted like nectar (nectar is when the food, the taster and the taste are one, lest you get any ideas about what that means and the last clear time I remember this state was when my mother used to make hot chappatis or Indian bread and serve it with a dab of clarified butter and sugar). He was humming as he cooked the Indian bread; the coal-fired stove still warm, its embers glowing from the deep of the oven providing a magical mix that included warmth, colour and sound. I was savouring the taste of the Indian bread and it all seemed just so divine. This space looked better than the cosmetic or sanitised dining hall for it had everything and, as I finished, he offered me a sweet from a box that had been kept, mentioning that one of his colleague's sons had just passed an important exam and this sweet was a part of the celebrations that were on. Perfect. I had no words to say but just smiled and folded my hands in a namaste position, thanking him for his gesture. He mentioned the importance of having a good meal before going to bed and the health risks of sleeping on an empty stomach. By the time I had washed my hands at the wash basin outside the dining hall and collected my room keys from the reception, the lights in the kitchen had been turned off and the old man and his team had made their way home from the back door. I walked back to my room, taking the stairs one step at a time, and that too felt good; just walking in silence, slowly, and watching each step and the unfolding of the walking itself.

This was just the first day in Varanasi and it already seemed as though the city had given me a lot of precious and yet very expansive moments. I had no idea how long I would stay there or what the next day entailed as there was no plan set aside to make 'use' of the tomorrow. I undressed in silence, the lights were turned off but I had a few tea-lights with me that I had brought along for comfort. The day had been unbelievably alive and this wasn't some meditation camp or course I was on but was just plain normal life and it seemed so healing. I wasn't thinking much of the day that had gone by or the day that was to come but was just witnessing the room and everything: a candle-lit room in the night with clean bed sheets, a slightly tired body and a well-fed stomach and sleep on its way to take me into another world where all the baggage was left behind. In that state, I lay on the bed, just watching everything, witnessing my eyes becoming tired of remaining open, my legs losing sensation and cooling down to a silent state and my breath slowing down to a beautiful hum. I never can exactly pin-point the time when the witnessing gave way to deep sleep.

Sunrise, a new day...many new possibilities

I was up very early as perhaps the body clock was still on GMT mode, but I suspect it was also that I had slept really soundly and now was the time the body wanted to get going. Breakfast at the guest house was served at 8:00 a.m. or a little earlier and it was just nearing 6:00 a.m. I decided to go for a walk along the many lovely campus roads and set about getting ready for a walk into the past. The campus was lovely, as it always was as I remembered it, and I could see smoke coming out of the hostel kitchens, the staff there fervently getting ready to serve breakfast to a horde of hungry students. There was also the odd milkman, pink-turbaned and astride on his cycle, making his way round the houses behind the hostels, providing milk to the households and then moving on to the next. The silence was broken by many a bird beginning its day and, in the distant fields or the many playgrounds that dotted the landscape, dogs playing a friendly game with each other or a story-telling of crows getting ready for an early morning field conference. This wasn't a 'campus nostalgia' trip although there were many moments of fond remembrance. The cricket ground at the end of the campus called the Kings Pavilion where I had spent most of the four years at campus playing cricket; the engineering halls which I rarely visited; the ramshackle tea shop near one of the campus gates which served as a watering hole for the then ubiquitous tea; the engineering workshops that allowed for some freedom from the dreary classrooms; and the hostels where a lifetime was spent. All that seemed pointless; I wasn't in the least interested in retracing the past – not one bit.

I have two dear friends in Pune, India, by the names of Bhuvanesh and Vinita and both of them were supportive of my journey and wanted to offer whatever they could to make it easier for me. The tickets were booked by their agent and they had also contacted a priest in Varanasi, asking him to get in touch with me in case I needed any help. As I was walking the roads of the campus, my mobile phone rang and it was the pandit (priest) who was wanting to know if all was well and if I needed anything. His call wasn't one that I had expected and so that too was a welcome inclusion to the day. We spoke for a while and agreed to meet at 11:00 a.m. the same day and that started another chain of events which would take me into even deeper levels of silence. Ramcharan had arrived a good half-hour ahead of schedule and was waiting for me. I had a shower, a change of clothes and a simple breakfast at the guest house and we left for our morning sortie. There were two other things that I was now very consciously paying attention to. The first was that I was wanting to leave a place or a set-up at least as good if not better than when I had reached it or used it for my own needs (washing the common bathroom or the toilet after use so that the next one to use it would feel good for no reason was one such new and conscious beginning). The other was that I did not want to wait till tomorrow for any form of completion. The 'thank you' and 'I am grateful' was best, I felt, shared in person rather than over a postcard or a phone call and one of the catalysts for this shift, other than the accident that I had, was the fact that the cook who had taken care of me the previous night was now on holiday and had left for his village. He would perhaps come back in another week or fortnight, who knows when, but now I had no way of thanking him other than telling everyone else of his kindness. It just did not feel right to postpone a lovely occasion to complete a moment by expressing gratitude.

Assi Ghat again...stories of a different kind, shocking but soulful nevertheless

Ramcharan started the rickshaw and off we went; Assi Ghat it was, as it was close to the university campus and we had a few hours before the pandit made his way to meet me at 11:00 a.m. or so. The ride was uneventful, bumpy and noisy as can be expected in Varanasi, but once we left the main road (this is a funny word in Varanasi as main roads in this city are perhaps 12 feet in width and the average speeds in the low 30 miles per hour) for some of the by-lanes that pointed to the ghat, it was all quiet and peaceful. The odd cow on the road did slow down the pace but everyone seemed to be adjusting to what was a seamless and formless system in a way and we too, our rickshaw and Ramcharan, were a part of that. I was blessed to be an observer.

The Ganges at any time of the day looks exquisite, although the river is dying from the now so evident rampant pollution from all the cities it touches that makes its way into its waters. The death of our rivers, the arteries of our world, pains me like no other. I won't go into that aspect here but do feel deeply that concerted action is needed to save what is one of the world's finest life-givers. Assi Ghat looked different from how it was yesterday in the morning: the river-front was full with many women bathing in what was, I was told later, a very auspicious day; the shops around the ghat were doing brisk business selling a range that included plastic containers for carrying the famed 'Ganga-jal' (water from the river Ganges) and all things associated; and the sound of temple bells pealing in the background. This seemed like prime time at the ghat and I first made my way to the flower-seller lady and thanked her for her generosity and settled the score by paying her for her goods and leaving a small gift for her son (a bag of fruits) and then headed back to drink a cup of tea from a stall at the entrance. Varanasi is also a haven for beggars, some genuine (down and out and no one to care, or perhaps even terminally ill) and some fake (escapists from the ravages of real life) and Assi Ghat had its share. There is, for the most part, an emotional drama that goes on either in a very subtle manner or sometimes in a very overt manner and the case here was no different. I was sitting in front of the stall next to a tree on a stone pedestal, sipping tea, when I was approached by a young child, perhaps five or six years of age, and he reminded me of my own children (the emotional drama beginning at its early stages and by all accounts the child was the senior actor or so it felt). I was about to hand over some money to the child when he asked for the biscuit in my hand. That felt even more like an emotional tug and I gave him the entire packet and the tea too and then felt like buying tea and biscuits for the entire line of beggars that were sitting alongside the small lane leading to and out of the ghat.

I walked up to the tea stall and asked the lady if I could buy tea for the entire group of beggars, to which she replied in the affirmative and suggested that if it was entirely possible, I could buy some warm food and serve that as well. While this may sound to some like a racket in the making, the lady herself was a hard-working woman and her gaze was full of contentment and serenity. She asked me to speak to one of the beggars, in this case the unelected leader of the group, a sadhu (an ascetic holy man) wearing black robes, ash on his forehead and with a trishul (a trident) in his left hand. I wasn't interested in any spiritual dialogue with the baba, nor was I seeking his blessings, but just wanted to offer what I could and move on. He was in the midst of 'blessing' an Irish couple (an Irish accent is hard to miss) and after that saw me and felt I was next in line for the holy ash dab on my forehead. He was about to begin his customary greeting, 'Alakh Niranjan', meaning 'I salute that which is unseen and pure', a mantra with a deep meaning for the address is to the spirit within, when I smiled and folded my hands in a namaste position. Before he could speak, I mentioned my intention to which he was very supportive and, in an almost reflex action, picked up some ash and applied it to my forehead and got up to walk with me to the nearest restaurant. The eatery was a simple one and let me count the number of parcels we would need.

The order placed, we sat on the bench in front and I asked him his name and why he was here, sitting at the ghats, living such a life. That was when I saw tears well up in his eyes and he answered by looking up at the sky, saying that he was just waiting for death to liberate him from the suffering he was going through. It was that very statement 'I am waiting for death to liberate me' that struck me like no other statement had in a long, long time. I mean, a heartfelt statement such as 'I love you' always stands out, as does a rank insult or abuse, but both generate a reaction of either liking it or hating it, which was all well and allows the ego to experience either a massage or mayhem. This, 'I am waiting for death to liberate me' was different in that it did not generate fear (not one bit for I was past that) but it made see my own life closely and those of others I knew well. What was I waiting for and what were most people doing on the planet other than getting entertained or running away from pain? I felt deeply that he had uttered those words just for me and it helped form an unspoken bond with a man I had not met until a few minutes ago.

He started by sharing that his life changed dramatically after his son met with an accident and he could do nothing to save him; the hospital visits, costs and prayers all came to nought and he was a shattered man after that. His relationship with the Divine was one of trust and he said he offered 'hope' to those who came to him for his blessings. He had no belongings except the clothes on his back and a few items (an incense holder, a tray for the ash and the like) and he lived at that site all the time. During the winter months and the rainy season he took shelter in a temple nearby and that was it; no television, no credit cards, no responsibilities and yet no peace. There really wasn't anything holy about him but rather something simple and bare about his life. We walked back to the narrow lane that was his home and office to offer what we had to the others that he shared space with and noticed a very old lady who refused to touch the food at all. She was bent so much in her backbone that she looked like a giant spider that had crawled down from its web and was searching for a safe place on the floor. The 'holy baba' shared her story with me that she was ailing and was thrown out by her sons. She was seething with anger and was living her shame. He himself waited patiently for her to calm down and then offered the food to her, making small morsels for her to eat with ease. This utter helplessness, seeing this sheer poverty so up and close, was not new to me as I had lived in India before and was a witness to many a sorry sight at road crossings and temple outskirts. What was different, though, was that I was not running away from the view, shutting it off or labelling it as another fraud (kickbacks at the lowest of levels) to trick hapless tourists. I just realised that each of the guys begging on the street had a story to tell, a deep pain they were nursing and just sensing their sorrow and yet seeing their simplicity (not one of them bothered or heckled me for any cash) made me connect to their humanity.

With that, we left Assi Ghat heading back to meet the pandit. When one thinks of a priest in an Indian context, one who can recite hymns and mantras and can conduct prayers, the picture that comes up is of one who is typically middle-aged, has a slight paunch and is given to speaking in monologues. This guy, Pandit Ravi, was different. He was clad in a fresh kurta and pyjama (an Indian summer dress) and had parked his bike at the entrance of the guest house. For all practical purposes, he looked like a post-graduate student of the university or perhaps a middle-level bank employee. He had a silent demeanour about him and given that we were introduced to each other by one of my closest friends who happened to have hired Ravi for a few religious ceremonies, it wasn't difficult to break the ice with him. He spoke about his background, his education and what he offered to those visiting Varanasi. I shared that I was on a search, a personal quest to find peace for many years (many lifetimes and countless eons perhaps) and that I was tired of the search, for in spite of all the efforts there was really no clarity. He asked me what I had explored and I shared that it began with simple yoga and paranayam (I was teaching this at some of the camps that I was attending or was invited to attend) to the real unknown, Tantra and all in between. While we spoke about the nuances of a few of the techniques, his approach was one of faith and surrender. He looked like a well-meaning man and he suggested that I conduct a prayer at a specific time at one of the main temples in Varanasi, the Kashi Vishwanath mandir (temple).

Kashi Vishwanath Temple...a prayer, bowing down to the Unknowable

This was a Shiva temple, one that adorned the banks of the Ganges and the most famous of the lot. Shiva, meaning 'auspicious one', is a major Hindu deity and the Destroyer or Transformer among the Trinity of Gods and, in the Shaiva tradition of Hinduism, Shiva is seen as the Supreme God and is also known as Mahadev. I won't go into the intricacies of Hinduism or of Shiva himself (there is a huge treatise by name,

'Shiva Puran', meaning 'stories of Shiva' which makes for interesting reading) for that would be just a diversion and a page-filler. Anyway, who wants to discuss more concepts?

The daily attention on Shiva for the quality that he stands for, one of mindfulness in the midst of polar opposites of all kinds, was always there. The Vigyan Bhairav Tantra, the starting and most comprehensive text of the school of Kashmir Shaivism, is a discourse between Shiva and his consort and is spread over 112 methods of meditation which include techniques of breath awareness, chanting, visualisation, sensory awareness and more. My journey into the world of Tantra had many occasions where the invoking of the qualities that Shiva epitomises was the first step before the meditation technique. The mantra 'Om namah shivay' (I bow to Shiva) is one designed to bring awareness to the supreme reality within, with Shiva as the inner Self itself. The chanting was a regular feature of my morning prayers. Varanasi, as mythical tales go, is the abode of Shiva and Kashi Vishwanath the main temple for his worship.

As you can see, the last paragraph has been a recount of what I had read and believed and was not really from my own knowing, and I was deeply conscious of the disconnection, the spiritual and religious babble that I was carrying in my head. All efforts had failed so far, Tantra and more (although there were deep glimpses), to experience the 'Shiva' (silence, absolute, no mind and a million other terms) within and all that was available instead was just a set of techniques, loads of knowledge and a few skills (intuition and healing in the main) to show. This 'invisible script' that was partly written when I was very young and partly picked up as a part of a 'seeker's' journey had to be transcended for that itself was the real baggage, the realisation of the real accident. What is more, I thought (!) I was wide awake in the whole seeking process. I was thirsty to die to the old; the throat was parched with sand and salt and an invitation to a prayer sounded like just the thing to do. My mindset of not resisting anything that came my way helped and I accepted his suggestion. We agreed to conduct the prayer ceremony on the very next day and he left immediately after that. Ramcharan was getting a bit restless for although he was happy with the money he was making, he wasn't driving me around and he felt he was not doing his best as a result. He suggested many a place to go to but I wasn't in the mood for any sightseeing or unconscious eating. In that state, I agreed that his role as my guide was over and that I would manage my travel in the city over the next few days on my own. We wished each other goodbye and it felt complete as I saw his rickshaw turn the corner and head on to another road. He was gone but had left a beautiful impression on my life and it felt good for no reason again.

A 3:00 a.m. rise, a long walk and a short ride...at the gates, waiting, witnessing

Indian prayers, especially in some of the larger and more popular temples, start very early in the morning and Varanasi and the Kashi Vishwanath Temple was no exception. I woke up very early and bathed myself in cold water using the bucket in the common bathroom, and the feel of cold water running down my head, face and body felt just great. While it was very cold outside (though not by London standards where I lived), the chill was not an issue at all for the water was colder and my body had already touched climes a few levels lower. The walk from the guest house to the gates of the university was a long one and while making my way to the gate, I noticed that some of the dogs that woke up from their light slumber (stray dogs sleep lightly unlike those kept as pets) were not in the least interested in barking. This was perhaps the 'Banaras' or 'Varanasi effect' for the city is very, very peaceful, operating at possibly far lower levels of intensity than the rest of the Indian cities. I reached Godwolia chowk (a crossing of four roads) a little ahead of time but saw many a pilgrim already queuing up for a 'darshan' or an audience with the Boss himself. A lady was busy sweeping the corners of each road while another was busy spreading what looked like some white powder alongside the road corners and gutters. I learnt later, when I asked a police constable, that the white powder was some horrendous pesticide meant to deter and perhaps kill rodents and other pests. The lady was using her bare hands to do the job and that felt deeply distressing. Her whole life was at risk and she was oblivious of that. She had vanished to some other corner of the chowk never to be seen again. The pandit arrived on his two-wheeler around 3:30a.m. and we set out to go to the main gate. His bike parked, we then walked down a narrow lane that twisted and turned every five feet and reached what looked like a queue of perhaps 100 or so faithful.

A few shops were open and were doing brisk business, offering all sorts of stuff for the prayer as well as a safe place to store shoes, valuables and the like. The security at the temple gates was intense and I was frisked a few times (the temple was and remains under threat from a few fundamentalist groups) and then we walked in. The temple gates had just opened and we were allowed in but, as is the case in most such settings, a mad rush ensued and there was a mini stampede of sorts. I watched the circus and was amused at the 'hunger' but lack of real sensitivity that most of the pilgrims were expressing through their behaviour and body language. This wasn't the norm, though, as there were many who walked in quietly to take a place to seat themselves in the temple courtyard. This was my first visit inside the precincts and with the help of my priest and his colleagues I was offered a 'dress circle' seat to view the famous early morning prayer. The entire process lasted for about 45 minutes after which a few groups conducted their own personal prayer. I was then ushered in for the prayer that was to be conducted by my priest and his colleagues. It was a long ritual with many things offered to the deity and my own state was one of just staring at what was in front. I had reached a dead end in my life, so much so that even the prayer ceremony that was being conducted by the priest and his colleagues was in a language not known to me (Sanskrit) although I understood some parts. The flowers were plucked perhaps the previous day, the incense and all the other stuff procured from some shop; there was too much noise and I was responsible for all that, for I was paying for it based on the desires I had.

It felt so overwhelming at that stage and I just knelt down in deep surrender, silently crying within and wishing to be free from the 'inner and outer' circus that was on nearly 24/7 other than when I was in deep sleep. A thread was tied to my hand as a symbolic gesture and to serve as a reminder of what I wanted to accomplish in the days, months and years ahead. That done and after paying the priest and his colleagues, I left for the guest house with a small bag that the priest had given me that contained a coconut and some Indian sweets (an oblation as a part of the prayer). The prayer done and now what? It had not changed anything really, not in a way that felt distinctly different although the sound of the bells, the chanting in the background and the smell of sandalwood in the temple all made for a heady feeling. That heady feeling couldn't be the real thing for it was created with a number of accessories and I was offering my senses a taste of all those. That just did not sit well with me; it did not feel 100% complete and in that state I walked back to the guest house, had a light lunch and just lay down on my bed in the dormitory, watching the ceiling fan and the half open window. One thing was clear though; I had submitted myself to the prayer and all that it entailed with all my heart and was 100% in deep surrender. The quality of that surrender was the real deal or so it felt. There was no better state possible beyond that, or so it felt, and that made the heart feel a bit lighter and I never realised when I drifted into deep sleep.

Passengers in this 'game' called Life...the journey is the only constant

The sound of voices woke me up and it seemed like there were a good dozen or so students in my room. Rather than get up immediately, I just lay silent, with my back to them, listening to what was going on and I could gather that they were exchanging pleasantries with each other. There were two guys who had made themselves comfortable near my feet on my bed and a few others were standing in the room. This was a dorm and so this is how it was supposed to be, that anyone with permission to stay could make use of the space. I turned around and sat up on my bed to see there a youngish guy, perhaps in his mid-20s, sitting on one of the beds and two older people who looked like they were his parents sitting on the same bed but a bit away. My own mind was now making all sorts of permutations and combinations: will they all stay, will they allow me the silence I was so keenly treasuring, will they have a regular stream of visitors? A short while later, I introduced myself to the guys and then learnt that the youngish guy was recovering from a motorcycle accident (he was in a coma for a few weeks and the accident had impaired his cognitive brain functions) and that his brother-in-law, a student at the campus, and friends had come to see him after his recovery at the local hospital. His parents looked old and frail but also relieved to see their son back in a normal state. Now this was one heavy emotional situation and the static in the room was palpable. The guy's father was an old man, perhaps in his early 60s, a retired employee of an aluminium plant in Renukoot, a small town a good 120 kilometres away from Varanasi, and the guy's mum looked like she was a housewife and a doting mother. Her gaze barely left her son's face and all that I could sense was an emotion of gratitude that she was silently feeling and expressing at the miracle that had happened: her son was back from the dead in a way.

I spoke very briefly about myself, just mentioning that I was a former engineering student of the university and that I had come to pay my respects to the city before embarking on the next phase of my life. My book of stories seemed so inconsequential compared to the trauma these beings had been through that I left it, my story, at that by concluding that, I healed people from their pain. This was when the father spoke and asked if I could speak to his son and say something that would precipitate a faster healing process. I had no idea what to do. This state of not knowing but deeply intending with the utmost of sincerity and an open heart, is a great one though. This is when all that is relevant is revealed; the resources that are needed to deal with what is are made available. I speak from hindsight but then, in the room, I just wanted the guy to feel empowered and believe in the possibility that he could recreate his own life. We looked at each other and I shook hands with him and in that moment felt his hand and his energy levels; his speech was a bit impaired, perhaps from the injury to the brain, and his handshake was a meek one, possibly from the overdose of medicines that the 'shrinks' would have experimented with. I felt that he, his parents and the entire troupe that was with him needed a shift in what they were paying attention to; a reframe was the need of the hour.

We shared a moment of silent communion, me and the guy, as I looked directly into his eyes and I sensed that he, just through the quality of his gaze, was alive and wanting a way out of the limiting body-mind condition, the limitation of it. I had read a few books on palmistry, and although a complete disbeliever in this art form, I knew of its impact on those that believed. The guy's palm conveyed, at least from what little I knew, that he was to experience good health and I shared that, mentioning that I wasn't an expert at all on this and that the heart of my work was in simple conversations. It was then that I told him that it was just his body that needed to recover and that his attention, the 'trim tab' or the power to focus his energies, was in perfect order. The moment he heard that, his eyes lit up.

The bag that contained all the stuff from the temple was opened and shared with them for I felt that here was someone, here was a family, that needed all the support it could get – medical, emotional and mental. Faith is a big word and carries many a healing power (placebos work for the same reason) and I saw the effect, the silent closing of their eyes as each of them took a small part of the 'prasad' (part of the oblation that is offered during prayers) and wished that the guy would recover faster. I saw him smile and, in that moment, saw his mother smile too, for she had seen her son smile, perhaps for the first time after the accident. The guy's brother-in-law was studying for a law degree and was in his final year and I could see him too, silently wishing that all would be well for his brother. After perhaps half an hour of simple conversations on the importance of a nutritious diet, a healthy lifestyle that involved regular exercise (yoga and pranayam) and an overall state of gratitude, I left for a short walk outside to allow them some space and quiet time.

Drinking tea is a national pastime in India and Varanasi epitomises that to the core; almost every road in the city has its share of 'tea shops' (I wonder how much business they do) and I ducked out for a cuppa. On my way back, I saw the guy and his parents leaving as they were about to board a rickshaw. I had come to accept that I would share the room with them and so this was a surprise. The guy's father stopped them from entering the rickshaw and I walked up to the guy and gave him a hug and shook hands with his father, wishing them good health and happiness. His mother was standing quietly, watching everything, and I instinctively bowed down to touch her feet when she held her hands over my head and, in a manner that is so truly Indian, wished that I see my dreams come true and that her wishes would be with me for all my life. The only person from whom I was used to hearing such words was my mother and before that my grandmother. This was different, though, for I had only met this family a few hours ago and here she was blessing me in a manner that was so personal. I saw their rickshaw leave the compound of the guest house and then take a turn to the main road. The room that I was in felt different when I walked in. This feeling is an indescribable one and, at one level, the feeling can be attributable to the memory of the family, their state and the conversations that we all had; this is perhaps a deductive effort, a scientific one. At an altogether different level was also the energy footprint that was left behind in the room, created by a combination or an alchemy of our personal lives and the unique situations that all of us were in, but the simple heartfelt connection that we had felt. Both explanations have their merit and it was a combination of the two that made the room feel much warmer, better and more homely than before.

There was so much unfolding, effortlessly at that, that there was a point in time when I felt the need to speak to someone I knew but resisted the desire to call and have a chat. The angst, the fear and the desperation was surging and I had reached here, Varanasi, and did not know what to do next. I was contemplating the idea of heading to Haridwar, another city along the Ganges but way up north. Haridwar is one of the first cities that the Ganges touches after it descends from the mountains and that city is known for its yoga institutes. By the time I took a cycle rickshaw back to the guest house, it was well past 11:00 p.m. and the city wore a deserted look. A ride in an open rickshaw felt good and the driver taking me back was a young man who ventured to take me all the way back to the guest house. It was then that I got a call from the priest who wanted to know how I was and what I felt about the prayer ritual that we had carried out. He was leaving town the next day and offered to come and meet me before leaving to see if there was anything I needed (Indian hospitality comes as a package deal when there is a friendly introduction), almost sounding like a local guardian. We agreed to meet the next day at 10:00 a.m. after which he'd leave to catch his train to some city he was travelling to.

Sleep that night was restless, for although the experiences at the temple and then back at the guest house were complete and fulfilling in their own ways, I still hadn't 'buried the ghost', in a manner of speaking, and the internal dialogue was switching on by itself, unannounced and loud at times. The priest came to see me at the agreed time and we sat on the lawns outside; the discussion was of a general nature but I sensed that he wanted to share something with me. We spoke about various meditative paths, but when it came to Tantra he was clear that it was a much misunderstood path, one that led many a seeker astray. In that vein, I asked him if he knew a Master who was well versed in all things esoteric, the prime among them being Tantra. That was when he spoke of a professor, a maths professor who taught at one of the universities in the city, who was well regarded as a wise human being and who I could meet. The problem was, he said, the professor did not like to be introduced and also did not hold any satsangs or open discussions. The priest shared some details about how the professor had helped him deal with a physical and chronic ailment through the use of chanting, focus and breath work. His eyes reflected a sincerity that only a seeker can know and I set my heart on meeting this professor the same afternoon. The priest did not hand over a telephone number or an address where I could reach the professor but just his name, the name of the college where he was teaching and the subject that he taught. That was some lead to follow but with my state of allowing, not rejecting or choosing what came my way, this seemed a gift and a thread that held promise. I had nothing else on the radar anyway and all that was perhaps possible was to take the train out of the city to some other destination; I was tired of travelling, not at the physical level but at a spiritual level. Armed with just that information, I left for the college after a light lunch. The meeting was to change my life in ways that I can't even describe and I bow down to the wisdom of my Teacher and the blessings of those who love me. In a way, I know now that this meeting had to happen only at this stage. Any earlier and I would have been either wanting to share, impress or learn but now my hands were empty and my head, reeling from all the 'sadhana', tired. There was no more petrol in the tank and it was time to jettison the car and all the stuff that was with it, and just walk; and walk I did.

Meeting my Teacher...an unexpected and an unbelievable moment

The ride from the campus gate to the university where the professor was teaching was a long but uneventful one and so was the walk to the college building where he was teaching. I asked the guard at the entrance as to the professor's whereabouts and was told that he was teaching. Something in my earnestness made a difference and the guard shared that the professor was giving a lecture right now and would be free in two hours. He also mentioned that the professor would leave immediately after his class and unless I managed to get an appointment with him, it would be impossible to see him. Apparently, the professor was a highly disciplined man when it came to timing and measured in his conversations. He was, I gathered, highly regarded not just by his colleagues but by many in the city and the country who came to him asking his advice on issues that concerned their lives. He was also given to bouts of temper as he did not like his time to be wasted; a well-known politician at the national level had visited the professor but was not given an audience as the politician had come with his bodyguards and had asked the professor to meet him at a desired location.

The guard wasn't dressed in any particular uniform (most such staff members working in that part of India aren't pliable to wearing uniforms as it perhaps signifies their role and there may be some social stigma attached to it) but just a blue-checked shirt and khaki trousers. He took a liking to me for no particular reason other than the fact that I spoke his language with ease. We exchanged a few details about each other and somewhere midway he offered me a cup of tea from one of the tea-boys making the rounds of the campus. He then suggested I go directly to the classroom where the professor was teaching the students and ask for an appointment. I walked up the stairs, walking against the wall as the handrail was absent; it looked like the local contractor had yet to fulfil his side of the promise or perhaps he was holding out to collect his last payment. It looked risky nevertheless and I was wondering how hundreds of students made their way up and down the stairs without any incident. Anyway, I reached the second floor and walked down a small corridor to come to a classroom that held perhaps 110-120 students, all looking intently at the board, and then I saw the professor.

He looked more like a visiting doctor at an eye hospital or something similar rather than a professor but what gave him away was the chalk on his hands, his brow and his trousers. The board was replete with some quadratic equations perhaps and he was about to start rubbing one end of the board when he saw me and stopped to look. He then walked towards me while managing a glance at the students who remained silent as we spoke. He asked me what I wanted and I shared with him my background and why I was in Varanasi and that I had heard about him and wished that he give me some of his time and attention. He asked me to wait for another hour or more as his class was still in progress and said that he'd see me in his office at an agreed time – 3:30 p.m. that same day. He then asked me to speak to the guard to show me to his office where I could wait. I did as I was told and before taking me to the professor's office, the guard and one of his colleagues invited me for a cup of tea outside the campus gates. The walk and chat with them was simple and without any intent but I could see that they had a huge respect for the professor. We came back a good 15 minutes ahead of the agreed meeting time with the professor and I was led across a long corridor on the ground floor and a room that was in front of the chemistry laboratory was opened for me to take a seat in. There was a power cut in the building so I had to make do with whatever little sunlight that came in. The room looked sparse and devoid of any luxuries but the books in one of the cupboards looked like they were hand-picked from a million titles. Here I was, in a dimly-lit room of a newly-built building in a college campus, to meet someone with whom I had no personal relationship or any qualified introduction, to discuss my life, the basket and the baggage within. I had no idea what to expect, absolutely no idea, but the breath was unbelievably calm and the general inclusion of all that was (the guard and his colleague, campus, the room and more), effortless too.

The professor walked in just after 3:30 p.m. and I stood up, wishing him namaste by folding both my hands in front of my chest. He asked me to sit down and he then took a chair himself, across the other side of the table, not before dusting himself of the chalk powder on his hands and trousers and drinking a glass of water from a bottle that was on the table. He asked me what I wanted and who had recommended him; there was almost an impatience in his voice but he was still fully attentive. I shared a few notes about my background and my search and what had got me to Varanasi and left it at that. He paused for a minute and suggested I come to see him tomorrow at the same time. He said that he'd make time for me tomorrow. I thanked him for his attention and left the room, walking back and on my way out thanking the staff member who had helped me. As I boarded the rickshaw to get to the guest house, I reflected on the chat with him and noticed that there was no drama, no emotional swings in his demeanour when he heard my story or any ego-based trip of wanting to explain his view or his background. A typical chat in the corporate world would have been filled with so much posturing and pretence, especially if it was a meeting for the first time. In the alternative world, while in the main the demeanour is one of relaxed observation, the tendency to impress or rush to a solution is high and I was a veteran by now at seeing such warning signs. He was just fully listening and 100% present to the room and what was going on. The silence in the room was also quite something; we spoke and we were also interrupted once by one of his colleagues who wanted to know when they'd be heading home. None of that made any impact to the silence that was always present in the midst of all that was spoken.

I was even conscious of my own state as I travelled in the rickshaw which was far more silent than before. The goings-on outside on the road, the traffic and the noise that is so typical in a city like Varanasi and the millions on the road going about their lives – all that seemed to be happening on the screen and, although I was in the scene, I noticed an almost divided attention that was not consciously arrived at, but just a happening that allowed for me to see everything and yet remain unaffected. That was something and it felt deeply relaxing. Sleep that night was also a deeply sound one and it felt good the next day. Instead of heading out to the city, I just walked the roads of the campus in the morning, handed over a set of clothes to a local washerman (mobile laundry) who'd deliver them the next day and then sat down to write what had happened so far. I left after lunch to meet the professor and reached his office a bit ahead of time. The chemistry lab in front of the professor's room was open and I walked in to see his colleague, the one who had interrupted our conversation, sitting on one of the tables. A general chat with him on many a topic revealed that he was a deep thinker and a simple man given to leading a principled life. It was then time to meet the professor and I asked to be excused and headed out to the room where we had met yesterday.

The chat...a real one

The professor walked in as before, at the agreed time, and after the same ritual as yesterday he sat back and looked at me; no words but just a simple and open look. His first words hit me like a thunderbolt when he said that if I continued on the same lines as before, I would either go mad or become blind (sun gazing and its effects perhaps) and I had to make up my mind as to which was preferable. We then spoke for almost an hour during which, at one point, tears were rolling down my face and I mentioned that I had done almost all that was possible: meditative techniques, scriptures, penances, extreme experimentation and more and yet it did not allow me a window into a world that I had had glimpses of. He then asked me what I really wanted and I shared that I wanted to know who I was, beyond the name, the money and the story that was my life so far. He mentioned that he had helped many a seeker on the verge of a breakdown or during one and that my situation was no different. He was well-versed in Tantra and many an esoteric art but did not want to share anything by way of distributing goodies. He also shared that he knew the way Tantra was taught in India and in the West and mentioned that the lack of a devotional element in many a teacher's technique was the one aspect that ensured its (the teaching's) limited utility. He mentioned the way to transcend this path and said that his Way was not about giving long discourses or offering programmes. He then shared what was right for me and I took note of that as a practice I would commence from the very next day in the morning. His suggestion was to begin the day at 4:30 a.m. and then commence the meditation techniques from 5:00 a.m. to 6:00 a.m. and that was it. Everything else had to be dropped and it just felt right too. He also mentioned that all that I had done so far would come back in its own time when it was needed and was relevant. I asked for his contact number, which he gave me very reluctantly but said that the best place to meet was his office, at the agreed time. There was really no other exchange; he was not interested in money or fame nor did he want to prove a point through an extensive dialogue. It just felt natural to touch his feet and I bowed down and thanked him and left.

As I was leaving, he mentioned that if I had the time I could go to a kirtan (a form of devotional rendition) at one of the famed temples in the city the next morning and also visit Manikarnika Ghat. There was no overt set of rules at all but to just practise what he had suggested, to lead a simple life (avoid all sorts of fancy meditative courses and books too) and to listen deeply to what felt right. He said that the time for experimentation was over and that I just needed to see and come home to what was already the Truth. He, in that same breath, mentioned that all this would become clear as I progressed with the practices and lived a simple life, devoid of mental afflictions (!). He mentioned that there really was no way to cut short the process for that itself, the search for a shortcut, was driven by a 'hopeful' mind. It just felt that a foundation had to be set in place, or rather allowed to form, and that meant that the ground just had to be cleared of all that was stopping free flow. The baggage had to go right then, at that very moment. The decision itself was enough or so it felt. A huge load came off my shoulders and, for some reason, my breath became even slower and deeper and the inner hum just perfect and in tune with what was outside.

The next morning I was up at the agreed time and, after a shower, set about the practice that I was instructed to do and it felt like a witnessing of the highest kind. This was devoid of any external accompaniments or, for that matter, any remembrance of any scriptures and more. There was just a silent witnessing of the breath with three kinds of chants, two of which were silent, that just seemed to manage a gathering of the attention on itself. I can't describe any more of this than what I have, but I knew instantly that I had touched upon what was right for me.

The kirtan at Sankat Mochan...sublime melody for the heart, hearing the inner bells chime

I left immediately afterwards for this temple, again not knowing what to expect. My visits to temples until then, especially to those when I was in school, were with my mother and the understanding was that I was just to follow what was told to me or, worse still, just watch, surmise and play it out myself. The latter was the main reason I was a reluctant entrant to most temples for the entire process seemed too contrived, theatrical and heavy with goods that it somehow never allowed for a silent state to descend. This time I was going because of a sequence of events, unplanned but just perfect, all pointing to the temple.

The shops outside the temple had yet to open but those selling flowers had started to open their shutters. This temple had witnessed carnage a year ago when a bomb was set off by some lost souls and that had an effect on the security standards; mobile phones and wallets had to be deposited at a stall outside and there was a light frisking too. It's a shame that places of worship have had to adopt such postures and it really puts into question the whole concept that is organised religion and its rituals. Anyway, I walked in and was greeted by a monkey, literally, for this temple has them in hundreds. The one who walked close to me wanted to see if I was carrying any eatables. I walked right in and saw that the devotees gathered there had assembled in two groups and were getting ready for some performance. It all looked so effortless as some of the guys picked up small cymbals, a few others picked up bells and sat in a circle around the one playing the dholak (a double-headed hand-drum percussion instrument) who'd provide the tempo. I looked at those sitting around in the circle and they seemed relaxed and getting ready for a ritual, in a way, that was about singing praises in the name of the deities. I had never heard a live kirtan before and this was a gift, given what had happened in my life and the crossroads I was at. An old gent, perhaps in his 60s, started the proceedings with a slow and easy flowing tune and the entire entourage, if I could call it that, followed. The tempo increased and lilted from the fast-paced to the slow to the really sublime. I felt like getting one of the cymbals myself and joining in the melody. One of the group members offered me the ones he was using and I then joined in the melody by ringing the cymbals without a care in the world. This form of devotional singing, the kirtan, is very simple in that the lyrics are just names of various deities and the tune, again, very simple. I won't go into the intricacies of the mantras that were being chanted as that would be just another diversion and perhaps a repetition of what I had read. Rather, I will stick with the unfolding of what I was witnessing, within and without.

I then joined the chorus by clapping my hands in unison with the beat and singing my heart out and then a few things started to happen. I noticed that there were tears in my eyes and I just could not stop the flow. It was raining, as they say, in bucketloads and I was delirious with joy for I was perhaps, at that moment, free of all the anxiety and fear and perhaps a million more afflictions; just free and it felt absolutely immaculate. This feeling, though, was not one that gave me any sense of accomplishment but I was in deep gratitude (and indeed, ever since then, am always) for the gift that had come my way. I was utterly humbled by the simplicity, the beauty, the originality and the glitter of the moment. My whole life with its ups and downs and with me in it, almost similar to clutching at straws in a storm, appeared in front and I was observing all that and also knowing what was missed in the narrow 'me-mine' state. My shirt was soaked from my chest down and it was difficult to sing along but it felt even more blissful to be a part of the process. I had never realised that rituals could offer so much as a possibility (not going into the esoteric dimensions of the process and its intent) and just remained witnessing it unfold. Some of the older gents looked at me, without disturbing the flow, in a caring way and one of them even went so far as to nod and give his blessing and approval to what I was going through. The kirtan went on for an hour or so and by the time we finished, I was finished, too.

Getting up felt different – lighter and freer – and as I walked back to the temple to bow down, one of the older gents who was walking alongside said that the kirtan was perhaps meant for me. The pure vibration of sound, sung in a devotional state, seemed to be working its magic for all the baggage that was, thoughts and more, seemed to have been cleared for an uplifting state to just be seen and felt. This seemed like a sure way to transcend the mundane preoccupations of the mind. The moment was unbelievably expansive as it lasted for the whole time the kirtan was on and while the time on my watch was moving ahead, my attention was on that which was constant, just the NOW. The body felt just perfect, aligned and detoxed; the mind was calm and I was, for the first time in my life, watching all this outside of a meditation event or technique. I had gone into deep surrender, just a letting go to the moment that was infused with sound and so much love. I started to see all those around me and in the precincts and, indeed, later in the city too, as divine beings, sacred beyond compare and each on his or her own journey.

Manikarnika again...warm glow, what a difference a day makes

It was time for a trip to the ghats, back to the burning pyres. After a light snack on my way to Manikarnika Ghat, I walked along the banks of the river, across a number of ghats. The light from the flames and the burning embers lit the faces of those around – workers, relatives and dogs. I was witnessing the site with a wide peripheral vision to include everything; the heat from the burning pyre closest to me was too much to bear, though. The direction of the wind was such that it was blowing towards the city from the river and, as a result, the intensity of the flames and the heat and the smell of burning flesh were even stronger. I saw a group of six or seven men sitting next to a corpse that was covered in a shroud, a few of them smoking beedis (a local Indian cigarette of tobacco wrapped in tendu leaves). I saw one of them pull out a camera; the group huddled all around the corpse when one of them opened the cloth and raised the head of the dead body so as to complete the photograph. It was a moment that remained with me and still does for I looked back at my own life and all the tendencies to be attached to the human body, my own to begin with, and then to all things form. The attention on the formless was rarely in a conscious manner, while the attraction and attention to form was always unconscious in its expression. The meditation courses that I had attended over the years (barring a few), at some level were such that form and time became the key anchors to the flow of the day and the formless forgotten or just revealed through gratuitous openings or acts of grace. My own eyes and attention, I began to realise, were always on form and that was a feeling I can never forget. It made me even more uncomfortable (the option of settling back into a normal and unexplored life was always there but it did not have any attraction for me) in that I saw that the rope had reached its end. I was restless but still present to the restlessness. The need to see a movie (get entertained) or read a book on spirituality (subtle entertainment too) wasn't there.

I noticed that one of the pyres was running short on burning wood while the one next to it was a raging wild orange. A worker at that site just walked across to position himself between the two pyres and used a pair of bamboo sticks to prod the logs loose and then shifted a burning one to the pyre that needed it. As a part of that, a few pieces of cloth that were entangled with the log moved as well. The sheer pointlessness of holding on to possessions was clear at that very moment, for all that was form was changing constantly and, in this case, before my very eyes. The time spent in shopping, preening myself with brands and goods, the attachment to all that and more, was all such a wasted effort anyway.

At one point, as I was watching a burning pyre I had a surreal experience of actually seeing my own body on it instead, the skin burning and the flesh on the bones of the body getting charred and the digestive tract being spilt on the embers below. Far from getting a nauseating feeling, I was just transfixed and silent. I was seeing many more visions, if that indeed is the right word for it, of many bodies burn, one after the other, on the same pyre but all having some or other quality from my life. Almost the entire range of human emotions could be seen from the perch where I was and I remained a witness to that. Children jumping from the edges of a high step into the Ganges in sheer joy; relatives mourning the death of their loved ones by sitting silently; a wood merchant quickly pricing his goods and feeling content at having earned his daily bread; a clean-shaven young man in a state of shock at having to perform his father's last rites; a cannabis-smoking sadhu lost deep in the mires of maya but perhaps in some illusion of semi-enlightenment; international tourists of all kinds with all kinds of emotions staring at the proceedings - this was as live a stage as I had ever seen or been on and I felt a part of it, completely. I felt the place to be sacred beyond compare and bowed my head in deference to such a spectacle. While the entire set-up was man-made, the interplay of emotions, the backdrop of the Ganges, the mythological significance of the place and sombre nature of the process (of death) made it seem like a setting from a different dimension – surreal in ways that words can't describe.

An evening prayer...Kinaram Ashram, followers of the Aghor path

That same evening, the 7:00 p.m. prayer at the Kinaram Ashram was another hugely uplifting and sublime experience. The collective mix of the sound of the conch, a few big damrus (a percussion instrument that is shaped like an hourglass) and bells, all while watching a fire burn within the precincts, was a potent one, enabling a high of a kind unknown to me. There is a pond in the middle of the ashram that is considered sacred and the suggested ritual is one where the devotees, those who wish to drop what is not working in their lives (mental afflictions in the main), are asked to take a dip in the waters and then leave the clothes that they were wearing at the time of the dip. I was always a sceptic of all such claims but what struck me as unique about the ashram was the way it conducted itself. The focus in the main and through the messages that adorned its many walls was one of waking up from the illusion that was life, waking up to a state free of desires and aversions. There was no deity or ceremony but just an insistence on being watchful, bringing consciousness to daily activities. The bodies of some of the saints who had lived at and nurtured the ashram were buried in the premises and yet there wasn't a 'graveyard' feel to it.

I just soaked up the experience totally and left after that. I also won't go into details about the aghori path to transcendence for that would be another diversion but it's worth a separate read, perhaps worth exploring for those who can be a witness to the aversions of the mind. It can be stomach churning otherwise.

The ride back to the guest house that night was quiet; the air a crisp, cold 10°C and the mood silent. I had to leave the guest house the next day as a premier of one of the Asian countries was to visit the campus and was stationed at the guest house. His entourage needed the entire space for security reasons and the staff at the guest house told me reluctantly to make alternative arrangements. My time inside the safe setting of the campus was over and it was time to move out, perhaps symbolic in a way. The next few days at Varanasi were meditative beyond compare and I could keep on writing about some of the silent states into which I entered but perhaps that is best reserved for another time, possibly a book on Varanasi itself. I moved to stay close to Assi Ghat at a simple hotel by the name of Haifa and spent the time just sampling whatever felt right. I could not meet the professor but his voice, his gaze, his grace and his guidance seemed to have had an impact on how my life was unfolding. I gave most of my possessions away to one of the cycle rickshaw drivers for the way he was diligent and punctual about his business and I took a flight back to Mumbai before heading back to London.

Over the next year, I made four trips to Varanasi and in each of the trips I had the privilege of meeting the professor who finally accepted me as his disciple on one of my visits. A visit to his house for the first time was another experience that I will never forget. He lived in a simple setting, a one room apartment, sparse but clean, and it was clear that he was visited by many. The veranda outside his door seemed perpetually filled with shoes and sandals of those who came to meet him and his engagement with them was simple, direct and over and done with in a short period of time. He took a special liking to me for I was a former engineering student from the university in the city and he said he liked my intensity and totality. I am still in regular contact with him and am blessed by his grace. He was and is extremely well read, but more than his knowledge of all things esoteric was his sheer presence and clarity in saying what mattered directly. What is also common with him and some of the other Masters of our times is his sense of humour, his ability to create moments of laughter in the seemingly most innocuous of situations. Over the months and years, never once was there any expectation of money or any favours to be returned. In fact, it was the other way round; I would be given a cup of tea and some sweets or snacks by some of his closest disciples. He is against any of us congregating together later and discussing life and stuff, for his view is that we were best placed in going back to our normal lives and seeing that to its fullest potential.

The infinite abyss or the endless dark night, the negativity that is the darkness itself, can be daunting and, itself, unseat many. It is here, in such times, that a Master is needed. A glimpse of the deep dark abyss at the wrong moment (perhaps during a drug-induced intoxicated state or a state of heightened sensory stimulation) can allow for an unconscious fear to arise and take root. A Master helps here too and I was blessed to have had such a gift at a time when it mattered most. It felt like it was a good time to return home and by that I mean home to myself, just where I was. There was no doing or any dependency for that to occur but just a recognition of what was already at rest within.

BOOK THREE:
The Present, The NOW

The Magic, The Miracle, The Mystery

A gust of wind
Shook a tree this mornin'
Leaves, they flew in gay abandon
A shower on my skin, a feast for the eyes

A gift, a blessing
Beauty in its ultimate dressing
I step out on the walk
The wind begins to talk

The Magic, The Miracle, The Mystery

BOOK THREE: The Present, The Now

It's such a short life we live; perhaps an 80-year lifespan of which the first 15-20 are just spent studying, preparing and the last 15-20 are spent waiting. Many are lucky to avoid health complications but, on average, productive life is perhaps about 40 years or so. Much of that is spent either complaining about the past (how the first 20 years were) or worrying about how the future will be. Rather, this tendency to fret or to worry or both is a habit that has now become an addiction for most. The 'don't just sit there, do something' directive heard during childhood at some level has become a silent mantra. We just can't sit still, we just can't remain with uncertainty, we can't trust a state of 'not knowing'. The desire to do something, be certain and be sure has become an almost rabid pastime. In the din that ensues, the silence within is lost. In the rush to do, to create certainty, the focus is on the 'how' and being in action (on the treadmill) is the main criterion that cuts the grade. As that takes on a life of its own, some 'on the road' milestones become points of discussion and watering holes, but whether the road itself is the right one is missed. The realisation 'I may be on the wrong road' comes late, too late perhaps for there are a million self-chosen traps or 'responsibilities' that have been willingly entered into, just to be a part of the landscape. If you are still reading this book then what I am saying perhaps does apply to you. If you feel strongly against what is being expressed, please stop reading any further right now and use the time in a more productive pursuit. Life is too short to waste. Who knows, your way may be different. Who knows, you may revisit this book at a different time and read it from here. If you are still reading this paragraph, then I would really invite you to last the distance.

The constant state of anxiety (what does the future entail?) and the nagging pain (incompletions of the past) unleashes damage on the system that was perfect to begin with. Relationships start to suffer (a drop in libido, a drop in subtlety); health starts to deteriorate (the odd niggle, the premature ageing of the body); food starts to taste bland (no sparking of the senses, no real sublime experience); what was taken for granted starts to become a prized state (sound sleep, a healthy digestive system, a fully fit constitution); the exploration of all things external increases even more (the odd affair or fling, the customary holiday to a new place); basically, endless ways to calm a now 'chaotically misdirected' mind. It's a hopeless battle against the current, for this tide is bound to head to the rocks. There are countless examples of fallen heroes, those who occupied the most prized positions, those who were revered by society at large, who just couldn't deal with the basic instinct within and fell by the wayside. Unless the fires within are quenched, there is no peace that can be known. Any march ahead on an empty stomach will, sooner or later, have to stop and give way to a primal need: hunger (of many kinds). So what is needed to quench the fires? For one, nothing is really needed as an input but rather much is required to be dropped. In that dropping, in that 'light-hearted' state, a clarity arises, one that is free of societal conditioning, one that allows a real witnessing (without interfering), one that enables creativity and one whose ultimate expression is a state of total well-being.

My own journey until the visit to Varanasi was one of seeking a solution, a spiritual Valium if you will, to still the waters of the lake within. That just dropped of its own accord and the sheer freedom from the perpetually 'thrown' or programmed state to one of just witnessing and allowing was an unbelievably blissful one. It was almost as if the attention (and the energy that followed it) that was on the outside – seeking, scanning and making sense of all that it encountered – was now just at rest, focused on itself; a reverse flow of energy seemed to be a constant feeling as I began to experience a feeling of relatedness with all that was.

Somehow, my whole life started to make sense and there really was no angst about anything at all. The pointlessness of holding on to many things that were cluttering the physical, mental, emotional and even spiritual states became clear and then started the process of just dropping all that was irrelevant. The beauty was, the more the baggage was dropped, the more there was space and freedom for full blown self-expression. Relationships, creativity and a general state of total well-being started to become even more abundant. The tiny speck of knowledge that I considered as my own safe territory, my own means to survive in the world, seemed ridiculous to hold on to; not only was it insignificant but the identification with that was the biggest illusion there was. The part that was not in the realm of the known was so vast, so whole and so rich and yet available in an instant; that seemed clear. All that was needed was just to get out of the way of what was already the case. This 'getting out of the way' was not by way of effort but by just witnessing and keeping attention on that which remained unchanged, in spite of the circus that arose and subsided at every possible moment, almost of its own accord. The intoxication was and is unbelievable.

BOOK THREE:
The Present, The NOW

Chapter 1:
Getting back to the roots

I felt blessed just to be alive and, what is more, my parents too were alive, healthy and had the same zest for life. Much had changed since the time I had moved to London from India. For one, they no longer lived together, preferring to stay in separate places (which was a wise thing to do for it allowed for personal space) and they were also much older (in their 70s). My childhood was in some ways traumatic and devoid of any emotional bonding at home. The vestiges of that imprint were absent; there was no body memory of what had transpired then and any remembrance of the past was akin to seeing an old album, the only difference was that the album did not seem like mine. I felt totally connected and yet totally disconnected at the same time. The pain associated with any of the old baggage was missing. I was having, and still have, moments of silent laughter when some of the old patterns made their way back to centre-stage but lost their hold on the audience (the one who was witnessing) and then just left the stage, not in embarrassment but in complete clarity that their 'game' was up.

Celebrating my parents and my life with them...the first rays of a new dawn

The possibility of sharing what I had gone through and, more importantly, the life I was living now with my parents, was a divine one. Just being with them in sheer silence, bowing down to the two souls who took care of me when it mattered the most, was a blessing I did not want to miss. A former colleague of mine, a lovely Frenchman, had mentioned in one of his silent moments that his biggest regret was he had not had the opportunity of completing with his dad, just saying the obvious but the most difficult words 'I love you'. That was something I was conscious of and it just felt the right thing to do to take my parents with me on a celebratory holiday. There were a number of places I considered but it was Varanasi, without doubt, that stood highest on the list. We had, the three of us, made the trek to that city a good 28 years ago when they came to see me off at the university where I began life away from home for the first time. My parents also liked the prospect of spending time in Varanasi as there was an air of mysticism tied to the city. My father had also given a commitment to his mother (my angel, my late grandmother) on her deathbed that he would visit Varanasi in her memory. I won't go into a 'past life and re-incarnations' discussion here as it's a waste of space and there is so much ballyhoo out in print anyway. Unless this life, the one in the present, is fully and totally lived, any discussion about a past or a future life is meaningless in a way.

Our tickets were booked well ahead of the date of travel but, as is expected in an over-populated economy, we managed to get one berth confirmed and the other two as provisional reservations to be confirmed against any cancellations. My parents were a bit pensive on the day of travel at the prospect of sitting during a 30-hour journey, but we had one berth available and my parents could, in the worst case, alternate and manage to get rest. I, however, was not at all bothered as I was allowing whatever was to flow our way just arrive without effort. I did have an earnest desire to see my parents travel comfortably and that was the limit at which my mind stopped. There was no control it could exercise on the outcome and so it just settled into the now. We reached the station an hour and a half before the stated departure time and were among the first of the passengers to arrive. A bunch of coolies were busy getting ready for a night-long kirtan session and the build-up was just intoxicating. I joined the chorus for a while and then left to board our train but not before thanking them for their hospitality. We were joined in our compartment by a slightly agitated and generally troubled-looking guy who was perhaps in his early 20s. He too was in a similar position to ours – travelling without a confirmed reservation and he had been given a provisional seat that was the same as the one my father had been given. In effect, if there were no cancellations he and my father would have had to share a berth and travel seated for the entire length of the journey. That caused him a lot of angst and he tried his best to talk my father out of the situation by suggesting that we look for a berth elsewhere. His nerves were so frayed that it was causing my parents some distress too, and it was then that I offered him a snack that we were about to have. That settled matters for a while by which time the ticket collector had arrived and was checking for bonafides. He looked at us and, without any expectations, allotted the vacant berths to me and my father and then moved our young friend to an adjacent compartment. We now had the entire compartment to ourselves and, with the curtains drawn, it was our private space for the length of the journey. It was the perfect setting for us to chat, relax into doing nothing or listen to our favourite music (bless Apple and its meditative products, especially the iPod and the miniature speakers). Here we were, three human beings connected to each other as a family and yet three individuals who were each on their own personal journey. I shared with them that all that was needed to make this trip memorable was to allow each of us to have our own space while still being together. There really was no need for being right or for expecting a certain behaviour either; three very ordinary people who were just utterly relaxed in their ordinariness. This is the closest that I can describe to how it felt.

The entire stay in Varanasi was unbelievably blissful. Whoever we met, from the hotel staff to rickshaw drivers to those selling food items, all were just happy to be of assistance and they expected nothing other than a smile of recognition or perhaps a good word. The countless small but miraculous incidents that we encountered along the way made me feel deeply that this trip was meant to be. If I was to bring alive many of the incidents during my conversation here, it would take a whole book to write about them. There is a book planned that will cover the magic that was the trip with my parents and I am in discussion with the publishers about it. Having said that, one moment stands out from the rest, a moment where we were, the three of us, transported into a world beyond the known. It felt as if the mind had just calmed down or, better still, just evaporated and in its place was just a seeing, a witnessing of all was happening and there was no effort of any kind.

Our last day in Varanasi began very early as we left to witness the sunrise on the banks of the Ganges. We left the hotel at 5:00 a.m. and reached the Dashashwamedh Ghat where our boatman, a genial-looking and deeply devout young man by the name of Gopi, was waiting for us, his boat ready. For some reason unknown to me I had brought along my backpack and halfway through the ride on the river, I realised that the bag contained a few incense sticks, a few candles and a matchbox, left over from the previous night. The previous night on the Ganges was a quiet one for us, as each of us remembered our life and remembered those who had touched us deeply and who were not in flesh and blood any more. My mother had remembered her elder sister, my aunt (as loving as any aunt could ever be) and my father remembered his mother, and I had my grandmother in my thoughts. Although the setting then was one filled with light and sound, as is the case with most such places in India, for us it was a silent and personal moment that brought us closer as human beings, beyond the social and biological relationships that we shared. The bag I had with me had the items we had partially used the previous night and, for no apparent reason, I requested the boatman to take the boat to the other side of the river from where we could see the city and then face the rising sun with the city as a backdrop behind us. Gopi carefully docked the boat on the sand banks and we all got down, one after the other. The sun had yet to show up but the sky was turning a shade of purple and deep violet with large streaks of white all over. The ghats, golden them all, looked magnificent as the river in the middle, the Ganges in all her glory, looked all silver. It just looked, felt, sounded and tasted magnificent; just unbelievably rich and perfect in every way. I just felt like worshipping my parents at that very moment. I asked them if I could conduct a small prayer ceremony, to which they agreed, and then I set about making a small circle in which the three of us sat in silence. In the middle of the circle, I made a small clay statue of a deity that my mother worshipped and also one that was at the core of all Tantra meditations (the symbol of the union between the masculine and feminine) and then asked Gopi to join us as well (he was our caretaker and was just so responsible in looking after our safety) as he was one of us. I chanted a few mantras, as I do during my morning prayers, and then knelt down to touch my parents' feet. As I stood up, the sight was just unimaginable. I thanked them with the deepest of gratitude for sheltering and taking care of me and shared with them that it was time for me to move on in my life. I shared that I had fulfilled all the dreams that they had set out for me and yet, for all these years, I was not sure as to what my purpose was in life. Now, after years and years (and more than that) of searching, I had just dropped into insignificance, into a realisation that there wasn't anything I personally wanted to achieve but just wished to be of service in enabling freedom, real freedom, in the lives of people. I asked them for their blessings for the journey that I was to embark on. There were tears in their eyes and in mine too and it was a moment that allowed us to transcend collectively all limitations, all societal conditions that had set the boundaries of how we had related to life and just be present to the sheer simplicity and magnificence of the moment that was. A melting of sorts was unfolding and I was drenched in that flow. The sun was about to make its presence felt and the sky had turned a light shade of red and white with a few orange, yellow and violet edges to it. It was as if a golden hue had spread itself wide and made us a part of itself. There were no thoughts but just a witnessing, a childlike innocence, of seeing all that was.

We travelled back to Mumbai by air and the witnessing of ordinary miracles occurring never ceased to amaze me. The dinner at home that night with my parents was one to savour for a lifetime for it was partaken in silence and in a very, very measured way; every morsel tasted like divine nectar that was made available to us. There is so much love, not only in the simplest of conversations with them but also in the unsaid.

BOOK THREE:
The Present, The NOW

Chapter 2:
Letting go of the baggage

There is so much stuff that we carry with us all our lives. Some of it is in physical form and most of it in a formless state (as memories). This stuff or 'baggage' is also something that at some level defines our personality, defines who we see ourselves to be and who the world at large relates to. With this baggage there really is no freedom to be, but to just continue with the effort of lugging it around and 'acting out' the part. The fear of dropping it and then having nothing else in its stead is a big one and most avoid that action. Sticking with the old allows for certainty, enables a continuity and a painful certainty is perceived as better than a blissful uncertainty.

I was personally done with the masks and the façade that I had carried over the years and, in a way, I was already living a life free of that but it was limited to those close to me and those I met as a part of my search. That living was so good that it felt natural to expand the truth to my entire life. The baggage had to go.

Completing the legacy...customers, colleagues, investors and more

I was on a business trip to Cochin with one of our clients then, the Sunshine Group, at their annual conference, when the truth started to become clear. This was one of the clients I had worked with in Mumbai and for whom we (the company and the team that I was managing) were assisting in setting up a four-star hotel in the suburbs in Mumbai. One of their directors (a 26-year-old but much wiser than his age) and I were engaged in a discussion about life and death and all things in between. The time was about 11:30 p.m., the conference agenda for that evening was over and we were having a chat, forgetting that there was a packed day ahead, when I spoke to him about what I saw ahead and what I was so clear about. His immediate response was one of silence and then a heart-led acceptance of what was so, and then he shared some of his aspirations and perspectives about life. That conversation set the ball rolling and I later spoke with one of their main directors, a dear friend of mine as well, about what was important for me and how I was wanting to ensure that their (his company) interests were looked after, regardless. What was common in both the conversations was that the response was very supportive and it allowed them to share perspectives on their own life. In spite of our relative differences in age, social upbringing and societal expectations, we connected at a very basic human level, devoid of masks, and spoke in a manner that allowed all of us to really know and acknowledge each other.

My colleagues at that time, especially the two with whom I was working on a daily basis, were two young professionals in their late 30s. Both came from highly reputed institutes, with strong careers behind them, and had joined for the dream that the company I was managing expressed. They wanted to be a part of it as much as being a part of a young start-up and here I was, ready to share that the game was over. One of them was already on the verge of getting ready to move on to a different firm and the other was supportive to the very end. They did see that my interest and attention on the business was waning (the circus of having to posture, cook up stories, get an unfair advantage against some of the competitors and hustle for business was just too much of a compromise for it was affecting what I valued dear) and there wasn't a way to strike a balance between the expectations on the outside and the deep longing within. I spoke to both of them separately and offered them as much support as I could, given the circumstances.

The investors who had backed me to set up the company knew that India was a tough market and the intricacies and nuances of real estate as an industry made it a 'last frontier to win' in a way. While the upside was always a possibility, the compromise needed was just too much and it wasn't something that I could do, even if I wanted to. It just felt suffocating and pointless. The accident brought all things to a head and the search revealed what was my song. I had to move on and it meant a sudden change of direction. There was an unspoken bond of trust that was always alive between us and I was deeply conscious of my responsibilities. The US investors were led by a very able businessman and a close friend who was supportive and yet firm in ensuring that their interests were protected. I offered them the possibility of future revenues through the hotel transaction and the other interests that we had. The UK investor was a large business group that had unfortunately got caught in the 2008 storm that was the financial meltdown and never recovered from its after-effects. They were now in receivership with a local UK bank but their former CEO, who had become a friend by then, was supportive for he too was battle-scarred and working for a different entity. My office in London too had to go as I could no longer identify with the original intent with which the company was set up. The team that was managing the office in London and their CEO, a former UK Olympic rowing team member with whom I shared many a moment of laughter, were very supportive and did all they could to give me as much time as possible. The conversations with my colleagues, the investors and those in London were tinged with a momentary sense of regret that I had let them down, but more than that was also a deep clarity that I was living my truth. With that out of the way, it was time to drop the other aspects in my life that took too much attention away from what was real. The beauty of truth, the silent communication of an open heart and the magic of a sincere gaze are such miracles that just can't be verbalised but can be known, lived and felt. This is how it felt when beginning the unbundling of the legacy that was, the dropping of all the baggage that had accumulated over the years.

Dropping books, cricket, chess...there was no need for any entertainment as life was so rich anyway

I had collected many books over the years, all in the Mind-Body-Spirit space and it felt natural to drop them off at the nearest charity shop. The Salvation Army had a store in Hanover Square and was the closest from my office. One afternoon, I walked to the store with a large Samsonite suitcase containing almost all the books I had and gave them away. The lady at the store welcomed the offer and I walked back empty-handed and free from the baggage. Reaching the office, seeing the now empty and free window sill, allowed me to glance at the world outside as I sipped a cup of herbal tea and just let the moment unfold.

The same weekend, I took my cricket kit – a large bag that had three bats, pads and the entire gear – to a local charity shop on the high street where we lived in Putney. I stood outside the store and kept the bag down and lit a small incense stick to signify a moment for me that was pristine and sacred in its entirety. I then closed my eyes in deep gratitude for all the gifts, the memories, the highs and lows that this game had bestowed on me and folded my hands in a namaste posture. I left after handing over the kit to the store and walked to Putney Wharf, a smart-looking place with a number of bars, and sat down at a lovely restaurant, Carluccio's, and ordered a glass of wine. That was done and it felt like a whole lifetime of memories had been erased from the hard disk and that too, just as it happens in the virtual world, with the click of a button.

I had also been an avid chess player earlier but now the game seemed pointless to me for it involved out-manoeuvring and outwitting a competitor and the aftertaste, almost always, was an unpleasant one. The few lovely books that I had I gave away to a charity firm. I just did not want to waste a single moment on wanting to win for I was experiencing a high beyond just being a winner. This felt like a time to share the magic that was within and checkmating a fellow traveller, even though it was just a game, felt meaningless. I'd rather laugh my guts off or perhaps have a cup of tea in silence with the traveller instead.

My life as an investment banker required me to dress in a certain way and the collection of suits, ties, shoes and all the paraphernalia that came with that life was also a huge baggage in my cupboard. The old attire just wasn't hacking it as there was too much pretence tied to it. That too had to go and I managed to get most of it sent out in small lots to the local charity firms, Trinity Hospice being one of them.

The cupboard looked empty, light and fresh and so did my life. 'Tomorrow' – the sheer addiction to that word is a disease, that was clear. For once, there really wasn't a 'tomorrow' that I was planning for, fearful of or greedy for.

BOOK THREE:
The Present, The NOW

Chapter 3:
Including all, rejecting nothing

Real clarity is seeing without interpreting, for the latter involves a judgment that superimposes itself on what is seen. The mechanics of the mind get in the way of the experience of reality; the mind, with its narrow self-contraction, seeing itself as limited as it chooses one extreme over the other. That then drives all that is created and all that is experienced. In existence though, everything is polarised by its opposite; the source of matter is emptiness (break open an atom and you have space). In life too, all that manifests on the outside is based on an emptiness within – a seeing. The two polarities are opposing yet in some strange way complimentary to each other. This was clear to me and some of the encounters (I use that word for it signifies a shift in a way, a giving up of a position perhaps, such that life would never be the same again) enabled a disengagement of the highest order. I wasn't searching for any specific skill or knowledge, for the sheer pointlessness of that was evident. The art of just being, witnessing without engaging, started to become a known state, one that was even more sharpened when I met some really lovely souls who operated at the highest levels of personal integrity and presence.

The encounter with Mooji, the exposure to Advaita...an experience of clarity, compassion and seeing

Mooji, for those who may not know, is a lovely soul who holds satsangs, all focused on enquiring into the nature of the Self. He lives in London but travels all over the world and has quite a following – seekers from different schools who love him for his simplicity, his humility and his direct nature. I had seen a few clips of his on YouTube and his voice and what he spoke about did touch a chord within. I was in London over one of the summer weekends and decided to be in his presence. The event was held at a simple setting in Brixton and, on reaching there, what was most beautiful to see was the order and silence outside the hall itself. There was a huge queue, perhaps a good 100-120 people standing in single file outside. I walked to the end of the queue, having parked my car a few blocks away, and waited to be led in. After a few minutes, the queue started to inch ahead and we were slowly ushered into the hall, but not before taking off our shoes and paying a small fee at the entrance. Those ushering the crowd in and also ensuring that the hall was being seated in an orderly way were doing a mighty fine job at managing a surge without resorting to any physical or emotional drama. I was at the back end of the queue and by the time I entered the hall most seats had been taken and there were just a few at the back and a few at the side of the stage that were available. As luck would have it, someone from one of the front rows left the room and I was invited by one of the ushers to take the seat. It was about 10-15 feet away from the main stage were Mooji would eventually come and hold audience.

The hall was completely full by now and someone requested the audience to remain silent. In that silence, Mooji emerged from the entrance and made his way to the stage. I had seen almost all kinds of teachers and Masters, some in flesh and blood and some in books. I was beyond looking at stereotypes and he looked as ordinary as anyone else and that felt normal. He was wearing a cream-coloured kurta (an Indian dress) and an olive-coloured shawl draped over one of his shoulders. He was wearing a beaded necklace but other than that there was nothing else on him. He sat on the chair reserved for him, a simple setting by any means, and looked at those in front, slowly shifting gaze, as if taking cognisance of each and every one. My attitude towards all so-called 'God Men' was such that I kept away from anyone who professed that he or she was a Divine incarnation or had a special connection with the Divine. That to me was plain rubbish. Mooji began his discourse, or satsang rather, by sharing something about the nature of Being, all simple stuff that did not require one to know the scriptures or any special language. He spoke from a simpler and more accessible place and the conversation was one that was beyond words. Someone later got up to ask him a question; it was the format that he would invite someone to come on stage who would then ask a question which was the reason for their coming to the event. Mooji would then, spontaneously, explore that question and engage in a reflective dialogue on what was so. He dealt with her question by having her reflect back on herself and who it was that was asking the question; the entire engagement to me, seemed just clean and pure. This was my first experience of Advaita and, far from the esoteric dimensions it is purported to have, it just looked so clear to me. There was a photograph of the sage Ramana Maharishi and one of another awakened being by the name of Papaji (Mooji's Guru). I felt drawn to what was going on, the simplicity of the entire space devoid of any circus and the direct nature of the enquiry. I had read books that were the transcribed speeches of the enlightened mystic and spiritual teacher Nisargadatta Maharaj, but that was a good twelve to thirteen years ago and perhaps I was just not ready for Advaita as a way of enquiry then. This time, after all the experimentation and the circus that had been going on in my life, it felt different and there was something beyond words that was being expressed and I can only label that 'something' as silence. Within that silence, all was evident; the blank screen, the projections on it and the observer. I liked Mooji instantly and made a decision to visit Ramana's place in India sometime soon when it was possible. A former classmate of mine, Subbu, who lived in the Fiji Islands, a seeker and wise soul himself, invited me later that year to Chennai in India to visit Ramana's ashram in Thiruvanamalai. I will come to that later but back to Mooji and the event I was at.

I had no agenda or question, although one aspect had come up over the past few months and in particular during the past year that was on my mind. I was experiencing, as a part of the meditation events and more, a very spontaneous existence and it felt really good to be that way. What was a concern at some level was that I wasn't making the kind of money I was earlier and the list of social and family responsibilities wasn't going away by itself. Just continuing on a 'soul-searching' trip that allowed for many a subtle life experience but one that could result in a dead-end, as I had seen with so many on the seeker circuit, wasn't one that I was up for. Yet giving up what was so beautiful, giving up this moment, was also impossible in a way. The earlier mind games were about winning in the corporate world with the primary objectives of making money and getting more certainty in life. This game or play, as a seeker, was about space, peace, silence and more and there was the immediate fear that this new game could lead to financial ruin. The capacity to engage back fully in the 'material' world without letting go of the beauty and the bliss of the 'spiritual' world was the dilemma and I was feeling it was time to bring the two worlds together. That desire, though, was borne out of fear; this became clear in the first minute of my conversation with him.

I was seated so close to the stage that it just seemed natural to walk up and ask him the question, which I did. The conversation with him to begin with was harmless and replete with moments of laughter, but behind all that he was fully present to all that was. His line was very simple in that he just wanted me to notice who was observing the material and the spiritual world and could I know that observer itself? That just threw me back on myself and then there really were no questions but just a silence, a humbling (for it was just not possible to verbalise anything, let alone share what I was tasting at that time and later) and a deep sense of comfort. I left the hall after that session but did meet Mooji at his home a few times and was really taken by his simplicity and the effortless way in which he engaged in any conversation. He is a lovely man and is doing great service to humanity by inviting people to just reconnect with their original state, a state of pure awareness.

Listening to Gangaji...one of her recordings

Gangaji is a teacher who holds audience in the US and in some other parts of the world and I had been to one of her talks a few years earlier. The talks seemed too nebulous and vague to me as perhaps I was looking for something myself but without having an idea of what that 'something' was. In that state, her talk (series of conversations) with those attending seemed a bit distant. After Varanasi though, and after the experience at the satsang with Mooji, some of what Gangaji was saying all along started to register and make complete sense. There was no effort in trying to follow what was being conveyed, for there really was nothing being conveyed other than just a pointing to the Truth. It felt all along that I knew it deeply myself and this, the opportunity with her, was just an occasion for a remembrance of what was already the case. There was one particular talk of hers, the fourth talk on one of her CD recordings, named 'Being in Peace' that I really felt was at a different level in the way she engaged. I must have listened to that recording perhaps a dozen times and it felt so clear as to what she was pointing to. The origins of the misery seemed so clear at that instant and from then on.

Adyashanti...a Zen teacher with a difference

Non-duality seemed to be the most clear of all paths although I can't even call it a path, for that pre-supposes that it is separate from others, whereas it transcends all paths and takes a totally different perspective on what this 'seeking' is all about: its genesis, the pitfalls and the knowing of the Truth. The teachings of Nisargadatta Maharaj, Ramana Maharishi and those who came after that started to make sense and 'seeking' as a passionate activity and a 24/7 pastime had given way to just witnessing. I had heard of Adyashanti through a YouTube clip that was mailed to me by a friend. There was one particular video titled 'The Enlightened Shoe' that just caught my attention. The simplicity and the direct nature of his speaking was such a refreshing change; it was devoid of heavy stuff, dogmas, do's and don'ts and a million other rabbit holes to go in and explore. It was all there, at that very moment, to just know and recognise the obvious. He seems like a lovely soul and although I have never met him, it feels like we are already related and seeing the same sunrise or sunset, in a manner of speaking; just the interpretation and expression of it is different.

The sage of Arunachala Hill...Ramana Maharishi

I wanted to visit this place and spend some time in the quiet settings of the ashram and was blessed when my friend Subbu invited me to join him for a two-day trip to Thiruvanamalai. Subbu and I were classmates during our engineering days in Varanasi and I liked his space and the energy that he expressed. He was living in the Fiji Islands to be close to his Guru's ashram in Naituba but was visiting India to meet his ageing parents and address a few other responsibilities. The opportunity of visiting the ashram with someone who knew the place, and with whom I had a high level of personal comfort, was one to treasure.

We left Chennai around 10:00 a.m., travelling in his car that was driven by a caring driver by the name of Suresh who was more concerned about our well-being and comfort than anything else. I noticed that he would slow down at places where he saw the odd pothole (the roads in Tamil Nadu are perhaps the best in India) and would then gently manoeuvre the car, half apologising for the bumpy ride. At a place where we stopped for a light snack, he was the first to get out and scan the line of restaurants to see which one was the most hygienic. Subbu had spoken of his friends in Thiruvanamalai, a married couple, Ravi and his wife Kavitha whom we'd meet, and was conscious that he did not want any intrusion in our journey together. In the spirit of including everything, I was actually looking forward to meeting them and was taken in by their simplicity, their wisdom and love. I sensed a level of abundance in their lives that was just so refreshing, from when we were honoured with a home-cooked meal to the walk around the Arunachala hill itself.

The visit to the ashram and then the trek up the hill behind was a quiet one in the sense that there wasn't much that was exchanged by way of words between Subbu and I and the silence was noticeable. The teachings and writings of the sage himself, encapsulated in three books titled *Who am I?*, *Self Enquiry* and *Spiritual Instructions* were simple and very direct in their orientation, much like what I had experienced when in the presence of Mooji and some of the other teachers on the path. The ashram too was very much along the lines of those teachings: a picture of simplicity and openness. Meditators from all over the world (the local cafés around the ashram had a range of cuisines to suit the tastes of those coming) would come and just sit in silence for as long as they thought appropriate and there wasn't any hustling from the authorities for any donations or a promise of any miracles. The place felt very, to use the word, 'satvic' in its expression.

Adi Da...the presence behind the media-projected personality

Subbu was and is a follower of Adi Da and had, a few years ago for some inexplicable reason, gifted me a book *No Two is One* which was a collection of Adi Da's talks. I had not read it with any great interest then but something in Subbu's presence made me want to ask him more about the teachings of Adi Da. I later came to read of some of the controversies that were surrounding him but it really wasn't of any interest to me. Osho was much maligned, Jesus was crucified, Socrates poisoned, Moses banished and so this wasn't a first of its kind. If I just listened to what Adi Da said or read what he had spoken without having any filter of any kind (for or against him), then his words carried many a message, but the main one was that ultimate priority of this life, of being born as a human, was to attain spiritual enlightenment. This may sound simple but his ability to cut through the noise and speak directly on issues ranging from sex to death and everything in between was unparalleled. I liked what I read and was blessed to have had the privilege of being introduced to his teachings by my dear friend Subbu.

I was at a stage where there was significant uncertainty in life and yet there was immense beauty. I was noticing qualities within people, those close to me, that allowed me to see them as evolving beings who were expressing their life through their words and gestures and that my tendency in the past of pre-supposing their stance was limiting me in my relationship with them. The other unbelievable gift of this state was that I was meeting new people and the quality of connections with most was at a heart level. There was almost an innocence of a different kind when meeting people that allowed for no judgment to take hold and in its place was just a clearing for new possibilities. That is sheer magic, for it was clear that I was the creator of my own experiences; through the inputs or perceptual frame I was seeing the NOW. The more it became a way to just naturally settle into sheer witnessing, the more the present became intoxicating. This intoxication was driven by the fact that the future was not known and with me focused on the NOW, I had complete freedom to create it the way I wanted. The other related aspect that became so clear to me was that when there was a personal agenda on my part, it became almost impossible to experience the intoxication, the joy and the bliss of the NOW, the freedom that it bestowed.

BOOK THREE:
The Present, The NOW

Chapter 4:
Deeply understanding, fully embracing and transcending sexual energy

Why understand, embrace and transcend? Why not headlong into it and why not just enjoy this human existence? If it were that simple, we would not have sex as a mental and pathological malaise that is so virulent across the world. The real issue is that intimacy as an experience and sexual energy as a force is rarely, if at all, understood and honoured by most human beings (men in particular) on the planet. What essentially starts as a biological stimulus becomes a mental curiosity later, an emotional attachment soon after and a rabid 'urge to release' state after that. Many use sex as an escape from the disappointments and pain in their lives, only to find that sex brings them more problems than it solves. For the select few, though, it becomes a deeply spiritual experience but, unfortunately, social overtones against this energy and its expression, a lack of guidance at the right age and a commercial world that is out to exploit those under the spell of this force (almost everyone), ensures that the darkness towards what is a divine gift remains.

Money (and the goods it can buy) and fame (and power) then become substitutes for an unfulfilled mind to set and achieve goals and thereby seek completion. The world in a way has gone mad; on the one hand there is pornography much on the increase, and on the other hand an over-expression of greed (concentration of money and power in the hands of a few). The latter applies at all levels, regardless of their socio-economic status. A curious mind, unfulfilled in its quest (of understanding sexual energy), will seek out other avenues for releasing its frustration and so money and fame (power) become obvious choices – ones that get instant recognition by society anyway. As a society, we worship and look up to those high up on the money and fame (or power) ladder; in a way, it represents our own shortcoming, something that we as a society haven't been able to manage. The journey that we are on though, a personal one at that, is in silence and utter solitude. The din that is outside may temporarily make us forget that silence, that solitude, but there is surely a deep longing that makes itself felt in moments that are truly our own, moments when the mind is at rest.

From sacredness to the profane...and a million mutations after that

Sex is never a problem for non-human consciousness, in animals and other lower forms. They are driven by pure instinct (to reproduce in large numbers but are timed biologically) and for them it is just a momentary sensation. There is no identification with the event but just an unconscious surrender. For humans, however, sex is experienced as an always present possibility (a pastime at some level) which takes attention away from that which is momentary. Yet, this very experience gives human beings a sense of timelessness where there is no past and no future but just a momentary now. That experience then drives an addiction towards sex. What is a biological and a sacred gift is then seen as a commodity that can be purchased at will and therein lie the makings of a grand tragedy that afflicts humanity. Religion and society as a whole also take a limiting view on sex and enforce that without a regard to its relevance and benefit to people; institutions (marriage) are created for it, advertisers exploit it. How can a human being be truly free under all these conditions?

This disease is so rampant and so under wraps that the silent majority remain under its grip and society as a whole either suppresses an early stage curiosity or strongly polices a later stage rabidity, the media getting into a feeding frenzy when the latter is evident. There are countless examples of senior leaders (from the political, business and religious environments) who have shown weakness and fallibility to this energy and have fallen off the high pedestal they were on. Under the external show of rituals – smart clothes, the expensive make-up and the cultivated sophistication – an animal lurks within, one that is alive and ready to emerge unannounced, as is evident by some of the examples that we see, those who could not understand this energy and were lulled into an animal-like state and who then fell prey to its hypnotic charm. Beneath the poise and the façade we are, in a way, totally out of control. Yet there is almost a complete ignorance and a 'figure it out yourself' mindset towards it that is prevalent in the world we live in; how ironic and tragic is that?

We have done well as a humanity with much that needs a factual understanding. Science has taken us from the depths (risks to human life) to the heights (the 'all supreme' specie on the earth) and its primary tool is the human mind. The mind sees itself as separate from that which it analyses and that approach does work when a separation is needed or a surpassing of what is in front, or what is desired. Sexual energy can't be analysed or overcome. The commoditisation of sex is but a poor and sorry attempt by the human mind to bottle and categorise it into understandable parts. The energy is such that it doesn't lend itself to such a dissection. It takes two to make the energy reach its full potential and that implies death; the surrender of the individual for the rebirth of the combined. Yin and Yang together constitute a whole and, for that, the mind has to dissolve, has to die in the process. Death, in a physical form, is anyway a taboo and this death during the process of deep intimacy is another opportunity that is missed out of fear. The ignorance continues then and manifests in other forms. Other desires take root instead to douse the hunger that is within but is never addressed. The quest for money, fame, power and more are all transmutations, in a way, of the same energy and there is no real possibility for the world, or any individual, coming to balance unless sexual energy is understood and transcended.

This is also very evident in the world we live in. There are yoga teachers with whom I have worked who were well versed in training their body into various positions or directing their breath patterns through sheer attention. I found that some of them had not yet transcended their curiosity about sexual energy and had dealt it with in a violent manner, almost suppressing it through body contortions. The situation within corporate environments too was much the same. Sex and sexual energy, understandably so, was never discussed, overtly or even covertly, because of its ramifications on career and related aspects. The incidences of corporate executives, especially those in power, straying away and finding themselves in a pickle, are just too many to make the point without a doubt that this energy is still a 'wild tigress', attractive, alluring and totally uncontrollable.

A silent state, a deep knowing silence, is the penultimate step before the last step into the inner sanctum, but without an emotional catharsis (which many a time has its genesis in a suppressed sexual energy), it is difficult to remain true to the path of being a silent witness. When the house is on fire, when termites are eating into the very foundation, any future structural plan or a set of techniques for silent sitting don't deliver the magic that they promise. Some may be lucky to transcend this step, that of mental and emotional catharsis, but for most it's an essential phase to go through. Before asking the question 'Who is in?' or 'Who am I?' it's important to know where you are and what needs attention. This is my direct and personal experience.

First the foundation...a deep dive into the roots

The Vipasana courses that I attended many years ago, and the daily yoga practices that I was on, did help to quieten the mind, but only just. It was only after being on the path of understanding Tantra and then knowing the meditative element that is so core to the interplay of human energies (this was the gift that unfolded in Varanasi for me) that a true witnessing of the fire within was possible. I also noticed that my body was beginning to show signs of reverse ageing in that the tone and the texture of the skin, the overall health of the system as a whole and my own sense of what was possible physically, mentally and emotionally had expanded. It has been a long while since I have fallen ill to seasonal diseases, those caused by changes in weather patterns, for my understanding is that the immune system is at a much higher level of awareness compared to earlier.

So, the big question is: Where does one start? An understanding is needed really. For one, it's clear that nature itself is not an event but an unfolding. Nature exists in reverse, from subtle to gross, while we see the gross first. The subtler aspects are missed, dismissed as 'baloney' or, worse still, acted against. There is also no way to control nature (harnessing the power of nature is one thing but altering its course is another; trying the latter has been shown to have significant side-effects as is evident) and the best way to be in harmony with its pulse. Nature, left to its own designs, is always in balance and provides in abundance what is needed to its separate (for the sake of the discussion, let's see them as that) parts. This energy is from the same fabric, the same intelligence that makes nature what it is and requires a similar approach to deeply knowing its beauty. I won't go into the modalities of how this is done for that is the subject of another book.

One facet of the diamond that is Freedom...an understanding of this energy

True freedom, which is what this book and my life is all about, is not just freedom from a financial sense but one that includes an unshackling of all physical, mental, emotional and even spiritual hooks – societal conditions that limit or hinder the knowing of truth. This energy, an understanding and a transcendence of which, is at the very foundation of achieving that freedom.

The question I am often asked is whether an understanding of the sexual energy forms an essential part of self-knowledge? My personal experience is this. It isn't necessary but it is certainly a huge help in being free of a curiosity that can otherwise sap a lot of attention. Biologically, we are born out of this energy (sexual) and it is the most basic of expressions that we as humans have.

Unless the base has been understood, vertical ascension (a shift in consciousness driven by a shift in attention), becomes an exercise in futility. It's best to know and surrender to this energy so that it then, of its own accord, remains back in fold to then allow for a vertical ascension. Expecting that vertical ascension, though, is a trap for then the mechanics of the mind are clearly in play. The other way is just to realise the futility of the seeking of the external for completion (mating) and the withdrawing attention to that which is unchangeable. Old age and a natural reduction of hormones (testosterone or oestrogen) allow for a cooling of the heat that is but the mind can then unleash hell, based on the illusion of a 'paradise' lost. A deep knowing helps in bringing sacredness to an otherwise unconscious process.

The risks of being exploited on such a path are always there and very high in fact and so one has to be conscious of personal boundaries and personal limitations. Enhancing the ability to remain a witness, so that there is greater clarity, helps in making the right choices. With attention back in its own fold on that which is unchanging and not given to the vagaries of an external focused mind ruled by sensory stimulation, there is deep peace. When the turbulence in the lake ceases to be, the still waters on the surface assume a tranquil shape that reflect a state of silence. Peace is what remains. Peace is what was already the case.

BOOK THREE:
The Present, The NOW

Chapter 5:
From rushing and grabbing to slowing down and allowing

It is a harsh world we live in. Home, school, sport and work environments are just arenas in a way, where all that matters is winning and the identification with the outcome of the game freezes us and creates an almost robot-like state, where flow is the first casualty. Originality, initiative, creativity, effortlessness and innovation are such powerful and liberating (enabling growth through obsolescence of the old) words but unfortunately remain as concepts that can be read about; they surely aren't ones to be 'learnt' through greater effort or practice.

Slowing down...enjoying the glide

The need for speed has become an obsession, a frenzy of sorts. This is evident across all aspects of our lives from fast food (instant noodles, microwavable pizzas that can be served in a few minutes) to instant communication (emails, SMS, voicemails) to shortened and personalised media consumption (YouTube, ebooks, blogs, RSS feeds) to health issues (liposuction, cosmetic surgery) to social networks (speed-dating, pornography) to corporate performance (quarterly results, daily trend analysis, day trading) and more. The list is endless, it's across all aspects of life. The need for speed has reached toxic levels and we have half-baked products making their way for consumption, products that have significant side-effects as well as long term consequences. In matters related to health, this is perhaps the single biggest cause for a spurt in 'lifestyle-related' diseases and with increasing costs of healthcare and an ignorant populace as regards nutrition, we will only see darker days ahead. The first casualty in this 'rushed' mode is that all that is seen or felt is a blur and the beauty of the moment is missed. Slowing down is a luxury that most can afford but the fear of being 'left out' is the driver that keeps the lights on.

Just allowing...a reverse flow of energy in a way

Flow is the absence of resistance; this is an experience most have when on holiday but I am referring to flow as an everyday, every moment possibility. Large parts of my previous life were about wanting to 'get' to a certain place or to a result and if what was desired did not materialise, then the desire was to 'get out' of that situation. The moment was almost always missed. This wasn't the case anymore, for the witnessing of the moment unfolding allowed for a settling down of the need to grab that moment. There was also a beauty in just witnessing the unfolding. There was nothing to do to allow for flow but to just get out of the way (there are many techniques to practise this 'getting out of the way' though) by witnessing what was. That (allowing) is the most difficult part for most, for we are programmed to think and act in binary terms; a yes and a no, a white and a black, a left or a right, fight or flight and the effect of a binary mindset is but obvious. There is never an experience of reality, never a true experience of the NOW but, in its place, is an expectation of what a future state should be. There is never a state of true rest that is known or, if it is, it's a short-lived experience that leaves an aftertaste that lingers and makes us addicted to avenues that give us a similar high.

A silent neurosis under way...a shutting down of flow

Both these combined (fear and greed), create a state of enervated neurosis; attention gets scattered on one hand (energy following attention) and there is a simultaneous overload of data on the senses. The system then just manages to perform at a superficial level ('just do it') and the inner voice or the deep human longing to connect, to find meaning, to contribute beyond the mundane, is lost. That is a tragedy for its after-effects manifest in many ways. The need to win at any cost creates an almost rabid mental state; a mind at war with itself. Corporate frauds, while they have been around for many years, have been on the increase and the scale is now even bigger. What is more worrisome is that now, with the advent and mass adoption of electronic ways to communicate, the chances of the system being at risk at its weakest link and being exposed totally there, are very, very high. The incidences of youngsters, at work or otherwise, taking inordinate risks when under extreme pressure to perform, are increasing and point clearly to the fact that all is not well with the system as a whole. Families and firms, their reputation under constant threat, suffer, as there is really no way to intelligently police all possible scenarios of risk. An overhaul of the system is due. That is clear. Relationships, work-life balance, a taste of the simple joys in life, real creative performance and more are all lost in the frenzy; the illusion continues. This is not tenable in the long run for the negative effects of such a state are already evident. The other aspect and the real tragedy is that the beauty of being in flow is also intuitively known and much desired.

Witnessing the play of polarities...disengaging from a 'predisposed' state

Life is just a play; a play of two halves. A Yin and a Yang, a night and a day, a female and a male, orgasmic without intent, just celebrating. In that state, the result isn't important but just the process, the play; the delicate balance between the two polarities, total freedom and total connection. In that totality, in that Oneness or the union of polar opposites, is the magic that is labelled 'Flow'. This may sound esoteric but it is actually very commonplace. When the mind is at rest, with the ego or the judgmental mind out of the way, what remains is just pure presence. The possibility of experiencing Flow is ever present, on offer every moment, some more than others. That possibility is truly available when one lets go of the need to 'grab' that moment, for it can't be grabbed. It is the delicate balance that happens as the 'limited you' disappears from the picture. The sheer bliss of slowing down to witnessing the unfolding of what is, is what allows for Flow to be a felt experience. This, then, isn't a state that is dependent on extraneous factors but rather intrinsic ones. When the mind is fully at rest and yet fully engaged to the intent, the outcome is just a continuum of the present.

Some of the spiritual teachers and Masters who I lived with and learnt from shared their gifts. Their life itself is a testimony to the possibility of experiencing Flow, not through greater effort, through even more machinations of the mind (it isn't and can't be an external target) but through just a gradual witnessing of what unfolds. The mind, the agitated mind, quietens down to then allow for pure intent to manifest. This is not a process that can be understood by pure logic, by mental analysis, for the work that happens happens beyond the mind, transcending it completely to reveal a far more expansive state than the limited 'self-contraction' that the mind identifies with.

So what are the benefits of allowing Flow? Top actors, athletes and those at the very cutting edge of their profession surrender to and crave for what is known in common parlance as 'being in the zone'. Many use intoxicants to enable that state. The side-effects on the body and the long term effects on the mind are toxic but they (those who resort to such intoxicants) do so, for they know the beauty of that state. There is, however, many a way to reach the highest witnessing state, a way to experience Flow through a series of steps, the mosaic of which includes a combination of silent witnessing, body movement, contemplative conversations and more. The resulting effects on attention spans, on the quality of creative output, on relationships and on life in general are unbelievably rich and expansive. However, this isn't just an event (the suggested techniques and its benefits) but should be looked at as an ongoing process, so much so that it (experiencing Flow) just becomes a way of life. The beauty of this state is that it is just our natural state and the process (the one that works) just returns us to a state of remembrance, of knowing that which was forgotten. It creates the pathways so that the mind is at ease (trusting the process) and that then allows for what is our natural and effortless state to come forth.

The miraculous and the sublime are always in the moment. A child is conceived now, is born now, a seed germinates now, a bird is in flight now, ice melts now, the sun has solar flares now; all in the NOW. That can't be a doing, for doing implies an effort to 'get somewhere'. Its just Being and that Being includes doing, so much so that that 'doing' (as an outsider were to see and term that activity) is so meditative that it actually is a continuous series of NOW moments. As one remains in a state of continuum (just Being) where time stops still, a vertical dimension (in terms of consciousness) comes alive; a shift from a horizontal plane to a vertical plane has taken place then. This can't be understood in a linguistic sense but known intrinsically. It's like knowing thirst or hunger or knowing love; words are meaningless. Manifestation as a quality is always a NOW.

Most confuse Flow with 'feeling good and relaxed' and 'being in control' but Flow IS, when you are not; when the mind is at rest in its own fold.

BOOK THREE:
The Present, The NOW

Chapter 6:
Rediscovering total well-being

Total well-being as something that is 'outside' of us and one that needs to be acquired or learnt through the reading of books is perhaps one of the biggest fallacies of the human mind. This mind-set is exploited to the hilt by soothsayers, companies and the like who sell 'feel good' products and services, ranging from the mundane vitamin supplements to the more exotic 'spiritual retreats' and everything in between. This is not to say that all in the 'well-being' space are charlatans; not at all, for there are countless well-meaning individuals and companies who offer very specific and carefully researched products and services. At the centre of it all though, well-being just requires two things: taking responsibility for it and bringing awareness to daily life. The more there is awareness of the NOW, the more there is well-being; that is clear. It is also clear that it (total well-being) is not an event but an ongoing and an unfolding process.

The body as a temple...worshipping the divine within

A unique instrument is already at our disposal, one that is supremely tuned to the NOW. It is a complex system that requires very simple input for its upkeep. That system is our body. Just witness a small child before it is fed much of the mass-market rubbish and see how it responds with striking intelligence, an absolutely natural and unpolluted one at that, to its needs. That intelligence gets watered down over the years and then starts a slow but certain and visible ageing of the body. Ageing is a natural process as the body comes in contact with elements (all of them) to slowly lose its original state. This ageing is accelerated by an ongoing and an unconscious abuse that the body receives when it's fed or exposed to stuff that is not in harmony with its nutritional needs. Food is seen as a sensory stimulant in such cases, without regard to its relevance to the demands of the body, the time or the conditions of its consumption. Most don't have much of an idea about how their body processes function and treat what is akin to a supremely well-primed automobile as a pick-up truck to ferry rubbish from one location to another.

Propaganda has become science. Glitz counts more than facts and hearsay is accepted over self-knowledge. Educational books were actually sponsored by companies and a brainwashing has happened over centuries and is still happening. They say history is written by winners; here, the future of nutrition and well-being is written by global food corporations and pharmaceutical companies, and the effects are clear for us to see. On the one hand we have food companies killing us with toxins (sugar, additives and more) that our bodies can't eliminate, and on the other hand pharmaceutical companies treating us like lab rats, experimenting with our bodies until the natural intelligence within is watered down.

Rather than be 'in' the body, most are 'on' the body, riding it like a horse that is dragged and whipped without a regard to its well-being. It may work for a while; certain situations may necessitate a 'fight' mode of remaining awake. As an investment banker at Goldman Sachs, I recollect having kept awake for a straight stretch of 56 hours without a break as some illusory war was being raged. Years of abuse finally takes its toll and the instrument starts to go out of tune (the horse just refuses to 'buck up') and breaks down much ahead of its naturally programmed time. It is totally possible to stop and noticeably reverse the ageing process by just bringing consciousness to what is being ingested. It requires a moment of conscious witnessing of what is on offer and the simultaneous witnessing of the body response, either by way of an affinity towards it or an aversion away from it. This is my direct experience that the body does respond with amazing alacrity for its needs.

My story with my body...a re-discovery of good health

My trysts with attaining a state of perfect health in the past were limited to making regular trips to the gym and 'sweating' it out. If that wasn't enough, I was also having the occasional massage to heal tired muscles as well as popping health supplements, all in a haphazard way and yet hoping that the body would be fine. A system tested to its extremes at all times will start to stutter and so was my body, giving in to the excesses of alcohol (the odd glass of wine every other evening or a weekend semi-binge), the recklessness with food (animal protein and that too in perhaps the worst of combinations with simple carbohydrates or highly saturated or, worse still, trans fats) and the disregard for meal timings. There was an almost blind eye turned to the body and its symptoms of unease. The occasional one that seemed too much to bear was dealt with through the popping of allopathic pills. I was treating the body, the system that it is, as a modular one, where parts could be isolated and then healed. It just isn't made that way and the intelligence within the parts and the system as a whole, that sacredness that can only be witnessed in deep surrender, was missed. The odd visit to an Ayurvedic doctor who'd offer his take on what was needed to get me into peak performance did not help. I hadn't helped my case earlier either for the inconsistency with what was being ingested was way too high.

I then set out on a quest to find out what my body really wanted for its optimum performance so that it could best serve the needs of the journey that I was on. It was then that I started an eight-week detox programme at home, starting with the colon, liver, kidneys, blood and lymph. I won't go into the modalities of what the detox programme involved for that isn't really important and for those wanting to try out a body detox, I would suggest that it's best to do so under the guidance of a good nutritionist. This detox was also supported by a well-timed exercise regime that was, more than anything else, a means to get the body metabolism rate to an active level. I had tried fasting a few times over the previous two years but had rarely gone beyond the third day, but this time I was determined to reach states that were unknown to my mind and my body. Then started a search to find the best and most therapeutic ways to cleanse the body which led to looking up all the diets that were on the market. Most, in fact all of them, are just so toxic for the body as they ignore the basic principles behind the functioning of the human body as a system. I was blessed to have been introduced to two sources that provided the most comprehensive view on what it took to return to good health. The first was a book, a bible in its own class, titled *The China Study* by Colin Campbell and the second was a company run by Dr Brian Clement. What followed was a miracle of sorts for I shifted to a completely vegetarian diet, vegan and sugar-free and started to experience states of energy I had never felt before. The feeling I had then and still do now was similar to the one I used to have when I was a child playing for the whole day, coming home for short meals but having access to an unlimited source of energy. The results of following a holistic and nutritive approach for a return to well-being were apparent as I experienced a significant amount of weight loss and this was supported by a proper exercise plan that included cardio as well as resistance training. Sleep patterns had become normal and the need to sleep seven to eight hours a day had given way to five hours of sleep. Hunger patterns were also very predictable and I was now eating between five and six small meals a day that were helping to keep the metabolism rate high and honouring the body needs for regular glucose. The body was performing just fine and my small meals during the day were like pit-stops to refuel it for the immediate needs that lay ahead. The intake was planned either the previous day or the morning before (being in the NOW is all very well but that does not preclude such a move. In fact, it allows for greater freedom to just remain a witness to what unfolds). The biggest benefit for me from all this was to see my kids adopt a healthy eating lifestyle which is now paying dividends in their lives and will continue to do so.

Bringing consciousness (listening to the needs of the body) to nutrition, physical movement and rest allowed for an even greater experience of good health. It was then that I started feeling a different energy state that the body was operating at, a different intelligence that the body was responding with to the stimulus it received. The body was rejecting food items that it wasn't finding suitable to its requirements and this response back to me was through some niggle or the other. The body is always in the NOW, alive, and responds with amazing intelligence, and the miracle that unfolds is just unbelievable.

The mind...from wide angle to narrow focus, from agitation to a state of rest

Dreams, desires, aspirations, attachments and aversions all arise in the mind; all ruses to miss the real and stay glued to an illusion that is the experience of life. The future of how life should be lived is showcased by MNCs and media companies and then follows an unconscious journey for most that is laced with comparison, covet and many a mental affliction. Attention then is mostly confined to the fixed, the gross levels; the mind and its narrow self contraction at work to protect itself. This is how it is and most miss seeing the trap and then are caught in a web of desires, fulfilment and frustrations.

When the mind, through a realisation and a deep one at that, knows the eternal and sees that the body-mind construct is just a vehicle for experiencing the NOW, that realisation just allows it to relax into its own fold, into the SELF. Then it becomes awake at a level not known previously and there is clarity and a general state of effortlessness. When the mind doesn't generate the chatter that reflects and reinforces a limited sense of self, when it expands to that which is the NOW, that which always is immortal (the NOW is always the NOW), then a new seeing happens: an access to other realms, other energy levels and more. This is a personal state, one that can't be explained but can be known. There are many techniques to just experience the NOW but ultimately all techniques will have to drop to reveal that which is already at rest, at peace. Just watching is enough; watching the inner workings of the mind without engaging. Then the mind retreats into its own fold, ready for use when needed.

My accident in London and then the deeper realisation later in Varanasi on the banks of the Ganges, seeing the burning pyres at Manikarnika, had made me quieten down as regards desires. In spite of having everything, the feeling of incompletion was always a niggling one. The circus of various meditation programs and events (all well-meaning but perhaps a tad excessive) and the 'highs' that followed made it evidently clear that happiness was not in chasing dreams (Maya), material or spiritual. When a desire is fulfilled, the body experiences a still state (as the mind gives up the anxiety and goes back into its own fold). That is when one experiences happiness for the weight is lifted off the shoulders, momentarily.

Emotional well-being...the experience of being in love

Emotions (thoughts or mental modifications that take the body as a host then generate a range of feelings) are the magic that is the combined body-mind response to the environment it is in. Emotional impulses are stored within the body as memories (and certainly as sensations, as the hormonal levels dictate what is experienced) that, many a time, predisposes how a human being responds to a situation. This is how it is with most and the extent of how much people are governed by their emotions is driven by how aware they are of the triggers that set those emotions and the resulting programmed behavioural patterns in the first place. Emotional freedom then is a state of watchfulness when there is a 'pre-programmed' way of acting out a response. The greater state isn't in fighting the urge but actually just letting it be and witnessing it dissolving into oblivion of its own accord. Vipasana is one technique that works wonders for those with a high level of emotional angst. Dynamic meditation, a form of cathartic meditation that was offered as a way to enable a state of no mind, is another way to expunge limiting emotions and witness the calm state that is revealed as a result.

I had been through all those processes and each had their place in the journey that was. The most powerful for me though, and a lasting one at that, is the experience of being in love. Sex is the ultimate hiding place for the Ego, its last bastion. Love is the ultimate death for the Ego, its last. Being in love is almost like a bathing of sorts, a bathing in a sea of bliss that just aligns the entire body-mind.

Spiritual well-being...just the NOW, nothing more, nothing less

Being aware is our natural state, for it is the only state that does not require any effort. Every other state needs effort by way of attention, leaving and settling on that which is outside. Energy then gets frittered away by scattered attention. Any form of entertainment, any form really, is a leakage of energy as the senses get hooked to that which is outside. Wherever it (attention) lands, that becomes the experience. An immature state of consciousness is when attention is on the outside and is then addicted to contact. Transforming the energy that is entangled in the illusion of life, to be still (remain a witness) is the way. Indulgence is waste of all gains as outward attention takes one away from the path of self-discovery. What you think you know stops real discovery. So the idea is to drop all crutches, all knowing, and then witness what remains.

Maya is about stimulation; attention being taken away to that which stimulates and the senses get attracted to that, wanting more of the same (or less, depending). This stimulation is either at a subtle level or an extremely gross level and what is already at rest within is completely missed. Drugs, intoxicants of all kinds from the simple to the deeply complex and from the socially acceptable ones to the ones that can get you behind bars, take you to higher planes or levels of consciousness for they alter the inner bio-chemistry. Such practices I label as 'spiritual diets' at work for they allow for a short term result (a blanking of the mind) but the mind does come back in a bigger, more ruthless way as do habits in the mental and physical dimension. Also in a drug-induced state, you are still there to describe the state, while in a deeply spiritual state beyond a point you have to melt and merge; there is no separation.

The search that led me to Varanasi was one that was replete with an intensity that was exhausting as it was futile, based on a greater illusion of some 'awakened state realisation' at some point in time. For so many years and perhaps more than those I can count, I sense a search had been on, seeking something outside of me for completion; for being at rest, for being at peace. That seeking I realise was just ego-based for I had, as the 'I', assumed a separation between myself and what I saw. That itself is the path away from the inner sanctum and then processes (meditation courses), goods, relationships, momentary joys, all become means to merge, a way to feel whole. Whether that completion is sought through food, intoxicants, relationships or achievement, it just is an addiction, an external itch, an avidya (ignorance) that is an impossibility to correct with more addictions. Society encourages many such silent addictions for it propagates a 'group think'. After years and years, I finally see clearly that this approach is doomed from the very start and will never fulfil. That time barrier kept the illusion alive though, and it was Varanasi that brought it to a close; a cessation of the time dimension.

There really is nothing to do. There is nothing to learn or no path to take to get your own SELF. You already are. It is in the unlearning, in the dropping of the baggage (limiting conditions) that one can know what is REAL. There is a delicate balance of the non-striving Yin energy and a very well directed Yang energy. In that state, there is total bliss, where there is no doing but everything happens by itself. That is the principle of 'wu wei'. Choiceless awareness is just that.

BOOK THREE:
The Present, The NOW

Chapter 7:
Witnessing the beginning

Our story holds us hostage to how we perceive ourselves and yet there is a new beginning in the realisation that we are not our story. The identification with our story, the association with the finite, the fear of change and the baggage that is the sum total of all societal conditioning, keeps us wedded to the limited idea of ourselves. We can't be what we observe, that is clear. The freedom in knowing that we are not our story, and that the story is just an interplay of thoughts and memories that defines and limits our expanse, is a huge one. The story has relevance in so far as it enables us to survive and fit into the world that we are given to believe. The real opportunity as a human being is to go beyond the limiting confines of the story. That is the real beginning.

There are many triggers for that trek outside (inward journey really) but, in my experience, it is almost always driven by a state of sheer frustration, resignation or perhaps deep suffering. There is, of course, the possibility of going beyond the known, casting off the veil of comfort through sheer clarity and innate wisdom but such instances are rare. The human mind isn't one to allow for such simple gifts to manifest. I was at a beach site in Mumbai one evening and was watching a beautiful sunset when an accident on an adjacent road took my attention. What was interesting to notice was that there were more people interested in watching the aftermath of the accident than there were watching the sunset. Perhaps we are programmed to react instinctively to fear far more quickly than we are to pleasure and beauty. The former perhaps is linked to our fear of death and our own mortality; the unanswered questions that remain, the meaningless explanations that seem to confuse more than comfort. The resolve to understand the reasons for suffering is a much bigger one then and any shock, any kind really, can provide the genesis for a deep search for finding our own Truth. Just reading what some of the books and those in the know say does not help, for that Truth has to be a known and felt experience. Without that, we remain in the world of concepts, forever analysing and theorising. It is comfortable to do so for it does not require us to take any risk but to just engage in a series of mental gymnastics. That too, just engaging in a 'conceptual dialogue', is fine but sooner or later the dryness of it will become clear. I do hope it does for you, if at all you see yourself as one with that style. The nectar that is self-exploration through direct knowing, through direct experience, is an unbelievable one. Imagine a state of freedom that is borne out of personal knowing rather than just out of 'possessions' and you can then well imagine the silence and the presence that the state entails. I do wish that you explore the boundaries of your life, your definition(s) of who you are and who you are not and begin to see what emerges. Many a symptom may point to the possibility of an impending search and all that is needed is just to be a witness to that symptom without rushing to douse it with a tranquilliser.

Symptoms of a larger crisis underneath the pain...just the tip of the iceberg is visible

Failing health, a faltering relationship, a loss of libido, a bereavement within the family or of someone close, a mid-life crisis – just about anything can be a possibility for going deeper into the real cause of the suffering. The opportunity is always there to challenge *status quo*, to go against long-held norms and rediscover what is already at peace within. That search, though, is one that is done alone, alone in the truest of senses. The possibility of a breakthrough is always there but the obstacles to that are also many: fear, envy, greed, lust and anger are amongst the main that lead that list. That possibility is truly available when one lets go of the need to 'grab' that moment, for it can't be grabbed. You will have to be it totally; you will have to disappear from the picture.

The mind is about senseless (unconscious) indulgence, either in desiring or being averse to (almost always unwillingly and without choice) an object of attention. These two extremes are serious hindrances to being in the NOW. Too much sleep, too much food or too much sex also end up dousing what can be labelled as an inner flame. Just a moment's watchfulness is enough to reverse the unconscious flow. There are many meditation techniques to allow for an experience, a window into that world, but techniques also have to drop one day, the moment when our true nature becomes clear. However, this realisation isn't a fixed position like a light switch that, once turned on, will remain that way. It's similar to walking the edge, complete watchfulness, fully in the moment, just being in the NOW without engaging and allowing all that is happening to happen.

From a religion of the masses to a religion of One...Freedom in its ultimate sense

A silent witnessing state is one that allows for sheer presence to be felt. That witnessing stage is beyond mantra chanting, beyond reading scriptures, beyond going to temples or holy places (surely not in the way that the circus is so evident, where rituals and noise have taken centre stage over surrender and deep silence). Religion, in the main, has become organised thuggery, set to soothe the senses and keep most in a deep stupor. Spiritual words, mantras and sutras have a lot of power; they are potent but when taken literally they lose significance and a new but essentially dogmatic religion is then born. Religion works on fragmentation of the individual; splitting us, creating duality in the mind (heaven and hell, us and God, good and bad) and taking away our power. It is perhaps something that is palatable to the masses for nothing really changes with religion; the way it is practised, the ignorance continues and the daytime sleepwalking is seen as the real thing. When we are fragmented, we can be exploited, as the first thing that arises with fragmentation is guilt. As a whole being, it is not possible to be exploited so there are vested interests as well. Some deeply meditative souls perhaps wrote their personal insights (awakening states), weaving them in stories that could be shared from one generation to the other and such that the essence was available to those who related to the stories based on the meaning (formless) rather than the form they conveyed. Unfortunately, the formless was forgotten for the form; subtle giving way to the gross and then all sorts of interpretations, confusion and conflicts arose. The Truth is one and in its purest form should really result in a religion of One, but we have over 300+ more and growing.

An unyoking from the conditioning...a return to innocence

This unyoking, a cessation of the separation, this fragmentation or narrow self-contraction between 'I' and 'Life' is needed. The closest that allows this as a felt state is Love but not love that is based on dependency. The other way to unyoke from the hooks that hold us to acting out pre-planned behavioural patterns is deep sleep, that divine gift which we have every night when we go into the unknown. That, however, is a body mechanism to allow for natural healing and renewal to take place. At a really simple level, nothing is needed for you are already that; when the baggage is absent, then the Truth of who you are is revealed. If that baggage is dropped in a conscious manner, then there is great celebration as that revelation happens; if it is dropped in an unconscious manner, as during deep sleep, then there is deep relaxation. Either way, without a dropping of the baggage there is just misery. Given the world we live in and the pollution that is so rampant in the food we eat, the music we hear, the air we breathe, the emotional conversations we hear or see or the circus that is made of the spiritual journey, the essential and the simple is missed; subtlety gives way to grossness. That is the tragedy, for the kingdom is lost.

The dark night of the soul is no big deal really...but a thought, a last-ditch battle of the self-contraction that is the 'I'

The dreaded state, that question in the unsaid 'What if I wake up one morning and realise that my whole life so far has been wrong, wrongly lived and now I am utterly alone?' That happened to me and I survived that prolonged nightmare, that fleeting hour that seemed like it would never end. That period seems endless and all that is hidden within and between the layers of the mind comes back for a macabre dance. At that stage, all knowledge becomes useless, worthless, as you are then set to the ravages of a violent storm, a rabid mind at its worst, attacking itself and there are no shores in sight, no safe havens. It is one of the greatest gifts that can happen for the next step is pregnant with immense possibilities. Taken rightly, you are intoxicated for life; the high is incomparable and a constant state. Taken wrongly and you can descend into the unknown depths of a vacuous existence. Grace is the gift of wisdom or a kind hand for the fortuitous step ahead. I faced that moment squarely, not in a confrontational way but surrendering and yet keeping my eyes wide open to see what was to be seen. Ultimately, there was nothing but me and the fear that was projected on the screen ahead.

Now is time to undefine, not redefine but undefine yourself...in an effortless manner

The miracle in your life has already happened. You are that miracle. Your birth, in spite of all the odds against you has happened, so stop seeking for more miracles and just be in gratitude that the real miracle has already taken place. It's one that required no effort on your part and you have had the gift of this life. As long as the 'I am in the picture' statement remains, the journey continues. Without the I, it's just the NOW, an unfolding, a seeing. The I, however, feels inadequate to be a part of the bigger expanse and prefers, rather adopts, a narrow self-contraction and that is the real tragedy. Now is the time to drop the baggage to discover what is REAL. It's the only journey that is worth making. You owe it to your heart and you have nothing to lose but your baggage. There is no seeking outside and yet that very seeking is necessary to get to that realisation. The search really begins with a complete acceptance that something is amiss, something isn't right and that all known ways to deal or sort that incompletion don't work. Then begins the real search to find a way to heal what is niggling but unsolvable. There is always a way ahead but it starts with a dead end. Find your path that will lead to your truth, to your own realisation.

Drop your baggage and know what is REAL. It's child's play in a way for it will return you to your original state. What greater gift can there be than this? What greater gift can you give yourself?

a: Walking on the edge: potential traps along the way

Seekers on the path of Truth are a vulnerable lot for they go with trust. The risks are many and so are the rewards for it is through total trust, in a state of complete surrender, that the Truth is revealed. The risks do exist though, and the biggest of them all is the risk of being led away from the path that is inherently simple to one that is replete with superstitions, dogmas and temporary highs. Such roads all lead away from the centre and the signs of that are evident when one becomes an 'experience hunter', seeking one meditation technique after the other. The descent into a vacuous state then is but a given and so is the need to be a part of sects and groups to experience belonging. The latter has its merits though, as there one does get many a pointer towards what may work but the thing to recognise is that this search, this quest, is a religion of one. Any more than that and there is a crowd, a confusion and the inner voice is missed for the noise and confusion that the outside generates.

I had my share of seeing the road head south when the inner navigation systems were voluntarily shut down in sheer trust and I am blessed to have had these experiences. In addition, I have seen some of the seekers who I felt were on the 'straight and narrow', lose their bearings to just descend into a state of vacuous experimentation.

The actor or the cheap magician masquerading as a Master...as a 'divine' re-incarnation

This is a game that is perhaps one of the saddest of them all, for it preys on the vulnerability of innocent seekers who, in deep trust, follow what is suggested and end up just missing the point completely. A new 'parent-child' relationship is formed at the subconscious level and it feels good to just 'surrender' to the feel-good factor and live life in an ignorant state.
The first experience was when I was around eight to ten years

old, when religion meant just following religious rituals that were suggested by those around. During one of the summer holidays, I had the opportunity of staying with my aunt's family who lived in an upmarket part of the city and who had an old gent, bearded and perhaps in his late 50s, staying with them. This chap was supposed to be a re-incarnation of one of the revered saints and was worshipped with flowers and incense. He was given to wearing white or cream coloured robes and did not say much but just gazed at those worshipping him. He had the first taste of the food that was prepared in the household and was offered the best room in the home to stay in, one that was en suite and with all possible creature comforts. I was following whatever the 'faithful' did but was sure that something was not right about the guy. He seemed like a harmless fellow but the sight of someone who had a real connection to the Divine (and that too as an entity outside) and we, the rest, were just minions, living out our karma, was just too much to stomach. I just played the part without letting it get to me. What brought matters to a head was when he gave me a ring to wear as my exams were approaching and the general view was that now I was blessed and all would be fine. As good fortune would have it, I flunked a maths test for the first and last time in my life just after that and, in a fit of disgust, I chucked his ring into a rubbish tip. That was the last I saw of him or made an attempt to be in his space. The last I heard about my aunt's family (she was a very loving soul) was that they had to sell their business and their house in Mumbai and set up base in a small town about 700 kilometres from Mumbai; a pretty downward spiral in a way for people who had this Godman on their side.

The other experience was a few years ago when, as a part of my search, I was invited by one of the teachers whom I had known for some time to an event in India, in Mahabaleshwar. There was a Japanese Master who was regarded as being 'enlightened' by his followers and he was holding a programme in India for those interested. In my blind and frenzied state, long before the trip to Varanasi, I decided to go ahead and be in the 'presence' of this supposedly enlightened Master. The five-day event was a harmless one in the sense that the meditation techniques were plain vanilla. The Japanese Master had an interpreter who translated into English what he was saying and I was half-dozing when the translated words shook me out of the semi-slumber. I shouldn't call him a Master anymore, so the actor said that his body was a host to many divine Masters to descend and that there were times when Jesus Christ himself came down to 'play'. It all struck me as incredibly ridiculous, funny and downright stupid at the same time. I was embarrassed to be there but there was this hope against hope that the teacher who had invited me would do her bit and even it all out. She was gifted and I was hoping that a bright spark would show up. It was the afternoon of the next day that I felt compelled to take this actor on, asking him in the room the source of his 'enlightenment' and why I should believe him. It was then that his acting went to another level, where he wanted to convey that some divine soul had already entered his body and he now wanted to rid me of my karma. The situation was both funny and untenable at the same time, for I had a tough time stopping my laughter and yet I did not want the teacher who had invited me, and some of the other friends I had in the room, to be embarrassed at the circus that was unfolding. I played the game, acting my part and when it was all over, left for my room.

The 'seeker' trap...addicted to drug-induced highs

I was in Jaisalmer and was on the rooftop of a hotel, watching the afternoon sky, when I noticed a guy who was on the adjoining terrace. We exchanged glances and a brief 'hello' when he came over the wall and shared some simple details about himself. He was a former MBA student of one the colleges in New Delhi and had just quit his job with a global engineering firm and was on a path to discover the meaning of life. He looked much younger than me, perhaps in his early 30s.

I don't know how music became the focus of our conversation (perhaps Jaisalmer is famed for its desert tunes) when he mentioned that he was staying at a hotel on the outskirts of the city called the Artists Hotel. This hotel, he said, was owned and managed by a maverick Austrian and the hotel showcased local musicians in live music shows, mostly informal, on every other evening. He invited me with much gusto and although it seemed appealing (an evening of listening to the music of the land), something seemed amiss. I accepted his invitation and headed to the venue at 8:30 that evening. As I neared the hotel, I heard the beating of drums that seemed like the one playing was in a rapturous and ecstatic state. The walk up the stairs at the back of the hotel brought me to the terrace on top, where the musicians were playing with absolute abandon, almost trance-like in their performance. The lead singer was supported by another musician who was playing a stringed instrument and it was very well until I met my host for the evening. He invited me to a table closest to the musicians and invited one of the musicians to come and play up close to me, almost a solo recital and a personal one at that. When I looked closely at the musician's eyes and then at my host's eyes too, it was clear that they were 'stoned' or perhaps on some other drug and were in a 'heaven may care' state. That set the alarm bells ringing in my own system and I left the place after making an excuse that there was a phone call I was expecting from London. The mind, in a moment's indiscretion, had jumped at the prospect of an experience (here it was music). I left the place and headed back to my hotel, reflecting on what had happened. Such risks remain and one had to be constantly vigilant.

Experience hunting...from one meditation technique to another, from one school to another

I have seen countless seekers who traverse many paths in search of that elusive, and yet always available, state of sheer awareness. The risk they face is that the experience itself becomes an addiction, much like a drug-induced high, and the purpose of the search forgotten. The mind has a million subtle ways of making this addiction look like it's not one but is actually helping the seeker gain valuable ground on the journey of self-awareness. It (the mind) works on the premise that there is a state to be found in the future, after which all aspects of life would be understood. The one thing to watch out for in such cases is the ubiquitous 'time barrier' that the mind holds in place for a state expected in the future.

Becoming a groupie...seeing strength in numbers and in belonging

This journey, that of growing in self-awareness, is a lonely one and can be highly debilitating, more so as societal pressures begin to mount as the search gets intense. In such cases, support groups (seekers of a similar kind) get together and allow for a common handling of the pressure. Whilst all this is good and perhaps a part of a larger design that isn't entirely understood, the risk is that 'group think' then takes over and the silent witnessing becomes an occasional act. One way to ensure that this (being a part of a group) does not sidetrack the search is to take time out on a regular basis to pursue what one sees as relevant. A teacher or a Master, too, at such times can be immensely valuable in helping steer the seeker clear of stagnant pools.

Escaping from it all...looking for a safe sanctuary

The charm of pursuing a spiritual path and of seeking the Divine within is a big one. This charm at times overrides the need to be responsible (carry out one's duties in the world) and then seekers on the path see this, the spiritual journey, as a soft option of living life. This is a real risk that can affect many a seeker on the journey inward. There are no guidelines that one can keep track of to be in balance between the material and the spiritual world, and perhaps the swing of the pendulum totally to the other side (spiritual) is warranted. The ability to discern issues that are clearly related to physical, mental and emotional health (well-being) is a very important one and needs to be nurtured, for many a time the trigger for a spiritual search is perhaps not a real trigger in its truest sense but just a deep ignorance or, worse still, a shadow that needs some sincere and scientific investigation. A close friend, or any truthful relationship for that matter, can be of great help in reflecting back the underlying reality.

Soothsayers on the path with promises...dealing with the noise

The truth can't be told as words are inadequate; it is already within, already the case, waiting to be discovered. Anyone who promises to show or tell the truth and 'liberate' you is just exploiting you and your vulnerable state. Just drop the shackles and stand completely alone in your utter nakedness and just be. See, feel, hear and taste all that is present at that moment, whatever comes up, and have no bridge between you and what you feel is outside of you. Drop everything and there you are.

b: Writing this book: in Jaisalmer, India

This book was conceptualised and written over a four-week period in December 2010 to January 2011 in Jaisalmer, a timeless and golden city in the north-western frontier of India. I don't know why but it just felt right to head to Jaisalmer. I stayed first at the centrally located Paradise Hotel on the fort, a hotel with lovely views of the sunrise and sunset. I then moved to the Raj Mandir Hotel, an upmarket and pricey one, as the former was seeing busy times. In the last week of my stay, I had the privilege of staying at the Garh Jaisal Hotel, the former residence of the King of Jaisalmer, at the south-western part of the fort.

In the course of the stay, I had the privilege of being assisted by some really lovely souls: Yasin, the hotel boy at the Paradise Hotel (who helped me from a potential disaster by picking up and returning my Blackberry that I had left on one of the chairs in the restaurant); Jai Kishen, the guy who manages an antique shop in the main square of the fort; K Parekh, a former Indian national rowing team member who runs an exquisite shop by name 'Light of the East'; Dalpat Singh, who runs a top-class eatery called 'Free Tibet' where I spent most mornings drinking cups of warm black coffee; Bunty, the local guide with a heart of gold, and finally the grandmother who owned and managed the Garh Jaisal Hotel.

Jaisalmer is unlike any city in India. It is a desert city that is a good five to six hours by road or rail from the nearest city that has a commercial airport (Jodhpur) and is about 130-150 kilometres from Pakistan. As a city and as a region, it has seen many bloody skirmishes over centuries, as Afghani hordes attacked Jaisalmer for its wealth and women and then settled in and around the precincts of the fort. The city, as a result, is a melting pot of various cultures, all living in harmony and yet in different locations spread across the entire landscape. I wanted to be in a cocoon of sorts, to just write without any external influence and this city provided just that. I rarely left the fort and was just immersed in what was unfolding every moment. The magical moments that began at the break of dawn, as the sun made its presence felt with the sky changing colours from dark and deep blue to violet and then white and all in between, continued throughout the day, till sunset. It was and remains a city unlike any other.

c: Glossary of terms

Various words used in the book have their origins in Sanskrit. While the author does not take an expert view on the words and their explanations, a short description is included here to give the reader an insight into their meanings and, thereby, the context in which they are used in the book. The meanings of the words listed are taken from a variety of sources. For a more detailed description of any of the words, the reader is advised to look up select internet sites that list detailed information.

Advaita
A path of enquiry that sees oneness as the fundamental quality of everything.

Alakh Niranjan
A mantra, a salutation that means 'that which is not seen, that which is pure'.

Ashtavakra Samhita
An Advaita Vedanta scripture which documents a dialogue between the Perfect Master Ashtavakra and Janaka, the King of Mithila. Ashtavakra Gita presents the traditional teachings of Advaita Vedanta with a clarity and power very rarely matched. Ashtavakra Gita states that there is no such thing as existence or non-existence, right or wrong, moral or immoral. In the eyes of the Ashtavakra, one's true identity can be found by simply recognising oneself as Pure Existence and that as individuals we are the Awareness of all things.

Avidya
Ignorance. In Buddhism it refers specifically to ignorance about the workings of karma. Avidyā is the root cause of continued involvement in samsāra and the experience of suffering by which one remains confused about the true nature of reality.

Bhagavad Gita

The Bhagavad Gītā, also known more simply as Gita, is a 700-verse Hindu scripture that is part of the ancient Hindu epic, the Mahabharata, but is frequently treated as a freestanding text. It is considered among the most important texts in the history of literature and philosophy. The teacher of the Bhagavad Gita is Lord Krishna, who is revered by Hindus as a manifestation of God Himself, and is referred to within as Bhagavan, the Divine One. The context of the Gita is a conversation between Lord Krishna and the Pandava prince Arjuna taking place on the battlefield before the start of the Kurukshetra War. Responding to Arjuna's confusion and moral dilemma about fighting his own cousins who command a tyranny imposed on a captured State, Lord Krishna explains to Arjuna his duties as a warrior and prince, and elaborates on different Yogic and Vedantic philosophies, with examples and analogies. This has led to the Gita often being described as a concise guide to Hindu theology and also as a practical, self-contained guide to life. During the discourse, Lord Krishna reveals His identity as the Supreme Being Himself, blessing Arjuna with an awe-inspiring vision of His divine universal form.

Chakras

Are said to be 'force centres' or whorls of energy permeating from a point on the physical body, the layers of the subtle bodies in an ever-increasing fan-shaped formation. They are considered the focal points for the reception and transmission of energies. Different systems posit a varying number of chakras; the most well-known system in the West is that of seven chakras.

Cobra Breath

Is a breath technique employed in a variety of Taoist Yoga and Tantra practices. It is a diaphragmatic breath, which first fills the lower belly (activating the first and second chakras), rises to the lower rib cage (the third and fourth chakras), and finally moves into the upper chest and throat.

Dorian Gray

The Picture of Dorian Gray is the only published novel by Oscar Wilde. The novel tells of a young man named Dorian Gray, the subject of a painting by artist Basil Hallward. Basil is impressed by Dorian's beauty and becomes infatuated with him, believing his beauty is responsible for a new mode in his art. Dorian meets Lord Henry Wotton, a friend of Basil's, and becomes enthralled by Lord Henry's world view. Espousing a new hedonism, Lord Henry suggests the only things worth pursuing in life are beauty and fulfilment of the senses. Realising that one day his beauty will fade, Dorian (whimsically) expresses a desire to sell his soul to ensure the portrait Basil has painted will age rather than himself. Dorian's wish is fulfilled, plunging him into debauched acts. The portrait serves as a reminder of the effect each act has upon his soul, with each sin displayed as a disfigurement of his form, or through a sign of ageing.

Dnyaneshwari

Is the commentary on the Bhagvad Gita written by saint and poet Dnyaneshwar during the 13th century, when he was 16 years of age. This commentary has been praised not only for its scholarly but also for its aesthetic value. The original name of the work is Bhavarth Deepika, roughly translated as 'The light showing the internal meaning' (of the Bhagvad Gita) but it is popularly called Dnyaneshwari, based on its creator's name.

Ghats

A broad flight of steps leading down to the bank of a river or lake in India, used especially by bathers.

Guru

One who is regarded as having great knowledge, wisdom and authority in a certain area, and who uses it to guide others (teacher). Other forms of manifestation of this principle can include parents, schoolteachers, non-human objects (books) and even one's own intellectual discipline, if the aforementioned are in a guidance role. Finding a true guru is often held to be a prerequisite for attaining self-realisation. In contemporary India, the word guru is widely used with the general meaning of 'teacher'. In Western usage, the meaning of guru has been extended to cover anyone who acquires followers, though not necessarily in an established school of philosophy or religion.

Karma
The total effect of a person's actions and conduct during the successive phases of the person's existence, regarded as determining the person's destiny.

Kashi
(Otherwise known as Varanasi, Benares) is a city situated on the banks of the River Ganges in the Indian state of Uttar Pradesh, 320 kilometres (199 miles) south-east of state capital Lucknow. It is regarded as a holy city by Hindus, Buddhists and Jains. It is one of the oldest continuously inhabited cities in the world and probably the oldest in India.

Kirtan
Meaning 'to repeat' is a call-and-response chanting performed in India's devotional traditions. Kirtan practice involves chanting hymns or mantras to the accompaniment of instruments such as the harmonium, a two-headed drum, and hand cymbals.

Kojagiri
A festival celebrated in India on a full-moon night in the month of October to herald the end of the rainy season and the onset of growth. The religious connotation is that the Goddess of Wealth is seen to be benevolent to those who remain awake through the night by showering them with her blessings.

Krishna
One of the most revered of gods in the Indian pantheon, he is portrayed as a charioteer and advisor to Arjuna in the epic battle, Mahabharat.

Kundalini
The energy that lies dormant at the base of the spine until it is activated, as by the practice of yoga, and channelled upward through the chakras in the process of spiritual perfection.

Mahabharat
Perhaps the world's longest literary work. It is eight times longer than the Iliad and Odyssey combined. It is considered a reliable source for questions relating to proper actions and social arrangements and the relations between the human and divine worlds. Mahābhārat means 'Great (mahā) Story of the Bharatas', the Bharatas being the legendary first Indians.

Manikarnika Ghat
Is the primary cremation ghat in Varanasi. It is one of the oldest ghats in Varanasi.

Mantra
Is a sound, syllable, word, or group of words that is considered capable of 'creating transformation' (spiritual transformation). Their use and type varies according to the school and philosophy associated with the mantra. Mantras originated in the Vedic tradition of India, later becoming an essential part of the Hindu tradition and a customary practice within Buddhism, Sikhism, and Jainism.

Pranayam
Is a Sanskrit word meaning 'extension of the prana or breath' or more accurately, 'extension of the life force'. The word is composed of two Sanskrit words: Prāna, life force, or vital energy, particularly, the breath, and 'āyāma', to extend, draw out, restrain, or control. This is almost always used alongside yoga as a way to strengthen and rejuvenate the human body and free the mind from mental afflictions

Prasad
A devotional offering made to a god, typically consisting of food that is later shared among devotees.

'Ram naam satya hai'
(The name of Ram is truth) is commonly chanted while carrying a dead body to the cremation ground in India. This recitation implies that the dead body no longer sustains the truth (breath) which is Ram Nam. The dead body devoid of the breath or Ram Nam has no value whatsoever.

Samsara
The eternal cycle of birth, suffering, death and rebirth.

Satvic
Serene, harmonious, balanced.

Shiva
Shiva is a primary Hindu deity, and is the Destroyer god or Transformer among the Trimurti, the Hindu Trinity of the primary aspects of the divine. In the Shaiva tradition of Hinduism, Shiva is seen as the Supreme God.

Sutras
Literally means a thread or line that holds things together, and more metaphorically refers to an aphorism (or line, rule, formula) or a collection of such aphorisms in the form of a manual.

Tamasic
Dull, lazy, dark.

Tamasha
Fuss, commotion.

Tantra

Has the connotation of an esoteric system in which exercises, practices and rituals are handed down directly from teacher to student by word of mouth, though often with the aid of teaching materials in the form of pamphlets and pictures. Any Tantra path is usually part of a system that was discovered, developed or established to explain, teach and initiate people into a radically different way of looking at, and acting in the world with the intention of experiencing Oneness that was beyond words and concepts. The esoteric, concealed, or secret part is often misunderstood as a reference to the intentional concealment of ancient practices. Some of these tried and true techniques sometimes rely heavily on symbolic or 'twilight' language. Also, there is little doubt that some teachers wanted to keep certain things from their competitors, and that there were times and political situations during which it was not wise to meet privately in small groups for any reason. However, the word 'esoteric' in relation to tantric information, systems and practices has more to do with the fact that they operate at a subconscious or subliminal level, below the threshold of everyday awareness. Without proper explanation and careful guidance, an impatient and unprepared person could really get into trouble with some of these methods. Attention was drawn to tantrism when some sexual aspects of it became known in the West. Unfortunately, and not surprisingly, this has led to a great deal of confusion on the subject. People incorrectly tend to assume that 'tantric' means something like 'about dynamic sexual technique'.

Tantra - Aghor vidya

Aghor is a term that means an absence of fear and is an inner state of being that is supposedly gained through the spiritual discipline known as Aghor sadhana. Vidya means knowledge. It is difficult to reconstruct Aghor's origins as the first practitioners on the path did not leave any texts or chronicles behind. The teachings of Aghor Vidya were conveyed from teacher to disciple to maintain its purity. These unknown sadhus didn't have residences and they wandered into the wilderness, lived in crematory grounds and paid visits to the sacred places to share their knowledge (medical, psychological, spiritual) with the masses.

Upanishads

The Upanishads are philosophical texts considered to be an early source of Hindu religion. More than 200 are known, of which the first dozen or so, the oldest and most important, are variously referred to as the principal, main or old Upanishads. The oldest of these were composed during the pre-Buddhist era of India, while some of the later ones show Buddhist influence and were perhaps composed after the 5th century BC.

Yoga

Yoga refers to traditional physical, mental, and spiritual disciplines, originating in ancient India, whose goal is the attainment of a state of perfect spiritual insight and tranquility. The word is associated with meditative practices in Hinduism, Buddhism and Jainism. Yoga is based on the Yoga Sutras of Patanjali, and is also known as Rāja Yoga to distinguish it from later schools. Patanjali's system is discussed and elaborated upon in many classical Hindu texts, and has also been influential in Buddhism and Jainism. The Bhagavad Gita introduces distinctions such as Jnana Yoga ('yoga based on knowledge') vs. Karma Yoga ('yoga based on action').

About the author

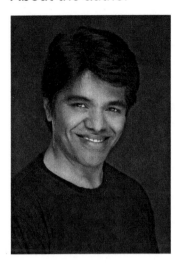

Rohan Narse, a former Goldman Sachs investment banker, conducts seminars, coaching events and exploratory conversations on rediscovering personal freedom in its truest sense, the knowing of which allows for an experience of spontaneity, abundance and personal power.

A chance accident in London, in which he narrowly survived, caused a sudden jolt from the 'programmed state' in which he was living his life as an investment banker and entrepreneur, that then created the context for a search for real freedom. He travelled extensively, seeking out many for their guidance, which finally culminated in a breakdown that took him in deep surrender to Varanasi, where he met his Teacher whose words allowed for a centering of the attention that was 'seeking', on itself. On the burning ghats of Manikarnika, he was struck by the deepest of truths and that set in motion a silent homecoming and yet a deep celebration in that very instant.

Two additional books currently titled 'Rediscovering Total Well-Being' and 'Absolute Creativity: Your Original State' are being reviewed and will be in print in due course. For more information on the books, the events and on social media related to Rohan, please visit www.rohannarse.com.

Rohan was born in India in 1965 and now lives in London, UK.

Lightning Source UK Ltd.
Milton Keynes UK
177650UK00001B/27/P

9 781907 722516